**FOREWORD BY LOU ENGLE**
FOUNDER OF "THE CALL"

# Invitation to a Fast

## MATT MADIGAN
AUTHOR OF 'THIS CHOSEN FAST' AND 7-14 BLOG

Ark House Press
PO Box 1722, Port Orchard, WA 98366 USA
PO Box 1321, Mona Vale NSW 1660 Australia
PO Box 318 334, West Harbour, Auckland 0661 New Zealand
arkhousepress.com

© 2019 Matt Madigan

All rights reserved. No part of this publication may be reproduced, stored in a retrieval system or transmitted in any form or by any means electronic, mechanical, photocopying, recording or otherwise without the prior written permission of the publisher.

Cataloguing in Publication Data:
Title: Invitation to a Fast
ISBN:  9780648507758 (pbk.) 9780648578000 (ebk.)
Subjects: Fasting; Prayer; Christianity;
Other Authors/Contributors: Madigan, Matt

Cover Design Maddy Barkley | Photography Ben Adams
Layout by initiateagency.com

For Alex
Thanks for the proofreading, Thanks for the example.

# CONTENTS

Foreword By Lou Engle — vii

1. The Power of Invitation — 1
2. Invitation to What? — 9
3. Invitation to Empowerment — 25
4. Invitation to Change History — 43
5. Invitation to do Justice — 55
6. Invitation to Die to Self — 61
7. Invitation to Listen — 71
8. Invitation to Freedom from Fear — 77
9. Invitation to be marked as the Bride — 81
10. Why don't we RSVP? — 85

Bibliography — 91

# FOREWORD
# BY LOU ENGLE

Some years ago I met a young man who was on fire for revival. He had imbibed my message on fasting, and with true hunger and great honor he drew deeply from my wells of history. He didn't just read or hear about my story, he began to write his own - not with a pen, but with a life of extended fasting. I am privileged to consider Matt Madigan one of my spiritual sons.

Years ago, when I first received the book *Shaping History Through Prayer and Fasting* by Derek Prince, fasting seemed to be somewhat of a side issue in the church. That book put a fire in my soul injecting faith into my heart that the history of nations could be shaped by the fasting and praying church. I never wanted to play for a losing team. I wanted to be a part of the ekklesia to see the gates of Hades challenged. Having lived out in some measure the legacy left by Derek Prince, I've seen the fruit of breakthrough fasting and prayer to shape the world. Not only that, I've been privileged to see hundreds of thousands, if not millions, uniting in prayer and fasting and believing for history-making God phenomena in the nations.

Now, today fasting is not a side issue. Recently I've been thrilled to run into men and women in Mexico, Germany, Canada, Ukraine, Russia, New Zealand and elsewhere, whose whole calling is to mobilize their nations into massive sustained fasting and prayer. What is going on? I believe it's the great fulfillment that Jesus spoke about when he said, "When the Bridegroom is gone, then you will fast." The fasting magnitizes the coming of the Bridegroom in all His power and presense.

Expectation of the coming Christ is creating a worldwide hunger for historic revival with fasting as the centerpiece. God is raising up voices who are trumpeting the sound of Joel chapter 2, "Blow the trumpet in Zion, call a fast… and in the last days I will pour out my Spirit on all flesh." The fasting is preparing the way of the fire of the Holy Spirit once again and these trumpet voices are initiating the sound. Matt Madigan is one of these voices who, out of the life of encounter and experience, is not content to remain blessed himself, but is impassioned to bring his nation and the nations into the public reward that Jesus promises those who fast.

With the sound of fasting on the lips of generals of intercession there will always come the questions, the doubts, and the critics - primarily from among the Church. Many raise very important questions concerning fasting. I am proud of this book. It is so well written and it answers many of these questions with well thought-out and articulated biblical revelation. I believe this book should be a key resource for those who are serious about leading the parade of history in fasting and prayer and mobilizing this last days movement described in Joel 2 and elsewhere in the scriptures.

I believe it is critical in these days that, as God puts his hand on certain prophetic men and women who are carrying this clear trumpet sound of united fasting, the wider body of Christ must discern these individuals' message and move in unified response to their sound. I believe that Matt is one of those voices.

It's time for more than prayer. It's time for massive breakthrough prayer, and the mightiest weapon of all is united fasting and prayer. Thank you Matt Madigan for being courageous as a young man and for casting your *bread* upon the water - both your *food*, when you fast, and your *revelation*, when you throw it out on the waters of history.

# 1.

# THE POWER OF INVITATION

The first time I saw it, it was like a momentary flash. I was not sure if it was real or just the product of an overactive imagination. My senses were now on high alert. My eyes peeled. I was now scanning moving hands and open pockets. Listening for the accompanying whispers. I thought I had seen movement but I must have been mistaken. I was often mistaken.

Of course it could have been possible. It happened in the playground often enough. This was a time and culture far removed from today. Today is a time when it goes out to everyone. The whole class. No special inner circle. But back then it was the close and privileged few. Being counted in their number was a position of status. The rest of us were the plebs.

There it was again. Now I was sure. The quickness of hand. The finger to the pursed lips. The muffled laugh. The knowing wink. I had seen the drop with my own eyes. The two agents would come close to embrace and then recoil. The secret envelope would be passed and just a quickly disappear. This was a era in which the invitation was limited. There was no idea of inviting the whole class. So whoever was hosting would slip and slink around the playground and with slight of hand conceal the drop. The idea was noble. To stop the plebs getting a whiff and the pang of rejection that that would elicit. But the noble gesture was useless. We would know. It was like a sixth sense for the *outcast* confirmed by the first envelope being hurriedly pressed into the open pocket.

This is a repeated scene in playgrounds worldwide. The date is set. The invitations are going out but only to a few. *Of course now as adults* it's easy to rationalise why we didn't get one, well, maybe easier but not necessarily easy. We understand limited budgets and limited space. But missing out of an invitation is not just a rational exercise. It can still elicit an emotion and still stings. We hear the echo of the school yard. It sends a whole range of messages not intended. It speaks of who belongs and who doesn't. The invitation has such implicit power. To the receiver it speaks of acceptance, belonging and place. To the non-receiver it is the opposite. Either way there is incredible power within that secret envelope.

**Story of the first invitation**

I can remember clearly the time that God started to make the idea of an invitation really clear to me. It was a few months before the first 40 day fast I did. I was emotionally straining over the idea because most of my Christian life had been centred on the idea of 'command'. It was clear to me that God commands. Many times in the Bible I had read it. Most of the preaching I had heard centred around it. What I really had little understanding of was the concept of invitation. The *two* ideas of invitation and command at first, seemed to be in competition with each other. Paradoxical almost. I was feeling drawn to the idea of the fast but wasn't sure if God was saying I must. I was processing everything through the paradigm of command. If God was telling me to do it, then I must. After all he told Jonah he must go to Nineveh and then tracked him down when he didn't. There didn't seem like much room to move.

So the idea of an invitation to fast snuck up on me.

I was grappling over this issue with my wife Kate and my pastor, Ken at the time. I believed it was something that God wanted me to do but the big question for me was; What if I fail? I was trying to come to terms with giving 'fasting' a go and seeing how it worked out. I wasn't sure if I would last one *day* let alone 40. So, as I discussed this with Kate and Ken and then spent some more time praying, I received what I believed to be the answer. God started to speak to me about 'invitation'. The idea was a revelation to me. Instead of picturing God as some sort of cosmic headmaster I saw him as my gracious father with hands outstretched, beckoning me to come and experience this thing with him. The fear of failure started to evaporate and a new sense of excitement flooded in its place.

That is part of my motivation for writing this book. I had a revelation that a kind Father beckons and he is excited by our response and that this invitation will transform the way we do faith. So in these coming pages we will explore what the concept of invitation does and how it transforms us. We will look at how common the idea really is in the bible and then how it transforms our concept of prayer and fasting from 'shoulda, coulda, woulda' to one of excitement and wonder. If you are really for such a journey, I urge you to read on.

## Change of Motif

Throughout the history of the Church, most Christian disciplines including prayer and fasting have been primarily thought of under the motif of 'command'. Instead of joy at the thought there is often dread, due to either internal thought patterns or external pressure. We always feel like we should be doing more. The little we do is never enough and so we beat ourselves up over the fact. Sermons on prayer urge us that we must pray more. In the long term the result is often not more prayer, but more guilt. Over the years I have spoken to countless people who talk about prayer in these terms. "I really need to be praying more" or "I must get more disciplined with my prayer life". The reality is that whenever we think about prayer and fasting in terms of "I must do more" we never will. When we reframe and say "how can I respond to this holy invitation?" then vast change is on its way.

There have been many occasions throughout church history in which fasting was imposed on the Clergy, by the Clergy or by the heads of State, mostly with terrible consequences.[1] This has mostly stemmed from an Old Testament understanding of fasting. On certain occasions in the Old Testament the people of God were commanded to fast. This however is not a complete picture of the Old Testament when it comes to the subject of prayer and fasting. There were also many times when fasting was not commanded but was done as a spontaneous response to a situation.[2] These spontaneous responses give us a valuable insight concerning fasting and invitation. Often 'command' will not produce spontaneous moments. More often than not 'invitation' will produce spontaneous moments. We don't really know what was happening in the hearts of God's people in the Old Testament as they decided to fast. It was probably a mix of duty and fear. However it is quite possible beacuse they knew stories of God's past deliverances, that they understood God's invitation to change the course of their history. They knew the heart of God was to relent and leave a blessing according to Joel 2.

This idea of invitation is not just limited to the Old Testament. It is my premise that what Jesus actually does with prayer and fasting is

---

[1] M. Black, *Fast of Feasten?* History Today, April 81, Vol. 31 Issue 4, p58

[2] Lambert, Fasting in Sakenfeld, (Ed) The New Interpreter's dictionary of the Bible 431.

rescue it from the realm of command and completely re-orientate it. 'Jesus refused to lay down any specific injunctions to fast' because he was concerned for the inward practice and not the outward.[3] 'Christ never imposed fasting'[4] and as such we can understand his re-orientation as an invitation to fast rather than a command. There is inherent freedom in an invitation to fast that aligns itself perfectly with the gospel of grace. This motif also aligns itself with the image of a bridegroom inviting the Bride to come to the final wedding feast and forever be one with the bridegroom. There is a lot to unpack about this idea. It goes against a lot of thought about Christian discipleship. However it is significant enough to change the way you view God and the way he wants to transform you. Are you ready to be challenged in a way that will change your life?

This idea of invitation will liberate your life. It will take you from "shoulda, woulda, coulda" and open up endless possibilities for your relationship with God. It has revolutionised my prayer life and that of others I know as well. In fact, I love this quote, which tracks the very movement I am talking about:

> *I was surprised, then exhilarated at how free I was during the fast. What began as a command quickly became a permission. The permission? Not to have to live on the level of my appetites. "Do not work for food that spoils," said Jesus, "but for food that endures to eternal life, which the Son of Man will give you" (John 6:27, NIV).*[5]

---

3 Blunt, Fasting in Hastings; Selbie; Lambert; Mathews, (Eds) Dictionary of the Bible 261.

4 Mentzer, Fasting, piety, and political anxiety among French Reformed Protestants 337.

5 B. Patterson, *Christianity Today;* 03/02/98, Vol. 42 Issue 3, p48,

The freedom that Patterson relates in that quote is an experience that many others have expressed as well. It has been my journey and that of others to whom I speak. The more you fast and pray in the spirit of invitation the more it becomes about responding to the call of the father.

## RSVP-less generation

Have you tried to organise a party lately? Or a night out to dinner with friends? Or even a social event for church? The one thing that all of these things have in common is that you really need to know how many people are coming. Whether it be so that you can work out how much food is needed or to book a table at the restaurant or even to book a bus. The standard thing to do culturally for generations up until the present day it seems was to send out an invitation and include an RSVP.

It's a funny thing, an "RSVP". It comes from the French *répondez s'il vous plaît*, meaning "reply please" or "please respond". Simply it means 'will you let me know if you are coming or not'. But it doesn't seem to be all that simple at all. Really what you are asking people to do is lock in a place and time to which they commit. It means that if something else comes up I have already decided what I am doing. This has been standard etiquette for generations. However it seems that there is a seismic shift in the way we organise socially.

Having four children has meant that over the last decade we as a family have hosted numerous birthday parties. Each year, about four weeks before the said birthday we will hatch a plan for the party and send out the invitations. On the invitation we write the acronym 'RSVP' and then set a date a few days before the event. The countdown then begins. Over the next few days we recieve some notes home from school with various children saying they can come or can't make it. We also get some phone calls. Either way we don't mind - we just need people to respond. But something curious has been happening lately. Some people simply don't respond. No letter, no text, no call. It's like the invitation just never went out. Even stranger is when they turn up at the event without having sent an RSVP. It's a little awkward. Worse still is when somebody turns up who wasn't invited. No, not really, I'm sure that has never happened. Ok maybe once. Now that was *awkward*!!

As I have seen this trend with my own eyes I am reminded of two things. The first is that it seemed to be quite different 20 years ago. Maybe it is not a new problem after all. Jesus even had the same trouble with a party he was throwing in Matt 22. It's just I have never seen it to the extent that I do today. It seems to be commonplace today that half of people invited to any one event will not respond in any way.

The second thing I am reminded is of is a book that I read some years ago by social commentator Hugh Mackay. The Book is called *Generations* and makes this insightful comment about the current generation. They

> *'Remain as non-committal as possible, for as long as possible'. Stability and predictability – even as goals – seem rather incongruous. Older generations are puzzled by the resulting reluctance to make long-term commitments to one course of study, one job, one sexual partner, one political party, one set of religious beliefs. What appears to be apathy or premature conservatism is more a case of 'making it up as we go along' – pouring passion and commitment into short term goals.*

So there is a shift that is happening and it means that RSVP is a thing of the past because you need to hold off on making plans for as long as possible, just in case a better option comes up. Or does it?

Mackay and others suggest the reason why RSVP seems outdated is that people are anxious to get the best. To go to the best party, to hang with the best crowd and to undertake the best adventure. It is not based so much on laziness as on fear. Fear of missing out. Our challenge then becomes one of demonstrating that there is no better option than responding to the invitation of the Creator. We might know this in our *heads* but often we walk the Christian walk and it looks like the heavy hand of command instead of the joy of invitation. The challenge then becomes demonstrating a lifestyle that is characterised by responding so deeply and passionately to the divine invitation. So much so that a RSVP challenged generation cannot help but be drawn in because they see it as better than the best they have been hanging out for. This is the invitation to pray and fast with such depth and joy that the invitation becomes infectious. So that those around can do nothing but respond with all their heart.

# 2.

# INVITATION TO WHAT?

Maybe you have heard the old joke about what the most important part of comedy is. The answer of course is *timing*. The humour with the joke however is that the joke teller says the word 'timing' without a pause and before the joke listener is ready to hear it. Comic genius they say. In the same way that timing is important to comedy it can also be critical to our spirituality. If you met a person trying to keep the law in order to be right with God, you might say their timing was out. We would say that system is done away with. It has had its time. It is really important to have our timing right.

The bible infers that we are invited to a feast. We read this and understand it from Revelations 19 v7. It says

> *Then the angel said to me, "Write this: Blessed are those who are invited to the wedding supper of the Lamb!" And he added, "These are the true words of God."*

The picture is of a future supper or feast at which the bride joins the Lamb.

Much of our understanding of this event is shaped by the parables we read from Jesus about a feast in Matthew 22. It begins

# INVITATION TO A FAST

> *Jesus spoke to them again in parables, saying:* [2] *"The kingdom of heaven is like a king who prepared a wedding banquet for his son.* [3] *He sent his servants to those who had been invited to the banquet to tell them to come, but they refused to come.'*

It is a fairly standard understanding of this passage to say that God is the King, Jesus is the son and the people being invited to come to the feast are ordinary people like you and me. As we respond we become part of the bride.

This feast that is spoken of however is a future reality. The invitation is true enough but it is for a time to come. So while it is correct that we have been invited to feast but we are yet to experience all that means. There are however Christians who use this parable as justification for a lifestyle of feasting now. Don't get me wrong; I love celebrating. I enjoy a great big meal with all the extras as much as anybody else but a feast is something else altogether. It signifies something has finished and we can now celebrate forever. In the Old Testament a feast would go for set days and then it was back to normal programming. This future feast will not conclude with going back to business as usual. It will mean time has finished, history has finished, labour has finished.

I love following sporting teams. I have my favourite ones and sometimes they even manage to make it into the Grand Final of the season. This grand final is the decider to work out which team is the champions. When I was younger I would be very excited throughout the game if my team was ahead on the scoreboard. It didn't take long to figure out that being ahead at halftime doesn't really mean that much compared to being ahead at fulltime. Can you imagine celebrating at halftime? You know, getting in the faces of the opposition fans and yelling your team is the best. You would be a fool. In the same way if all we do now is feast in anticipation of fulltime we forget there is still a job half done. To get into excessive feasting now is like celebrating a halftime lead. It's not time yet. We can taste it and see it but there is still work to be done.

So timing is important. So if we aren't called to feast just yet what are we called to? Great question! The bride is called to get ready for the feast by the lifestyle of the fast. Jesus spoke about this in Mark 2:18-22. It is a critical passage in terms of knowing the timing for things.

### They will fast 'in that Day'.

In Mark 2: 18-22 Jesus is questioned by two ascetic groups as to why they were fasting but Jesus and his disciples were not.[6] Ascetic groups were ones that have a basic spiritual DNA of fasting and going without the luxuries of life. Often they would go and live in the desert to escape the trapping of the city. The basic idea being that discipline was enhanced by fasting and the flesh could be controlled. The question to Jesus comes across as very bold and almost rude. It is almost like they are saying to Jesus 'we are spiritual but it doesn't appear that you are'. We see first hand what a religious attitude to fasting can produce. Being able to fast can so easily produce a self righteous attitude in us. It is like we can cross of a few acts of discipline on our spiritual to-do list and then we start congratulating ourselves and move into a religious spirit. It is the very same attitude Jesus is addressing in the Sermon on the Mount when he said to the crowd not to do anything for the cheering of man but rather the cheering of God.

If you discount any religious pretence from the question asker then this inquiry becomes a fair question as Jesus had recently done two things that seemed to encourage fasting. He had previously taught about

---

6 Garland, *Mark in Zondervan Illustrated Bible backgrounds commentary* 222.

the 'new' type of fasting in the Sermon on the Mount and he himself had just fasted for 40 days. So Jesus not fasting would have been quite puzzling. A little bit like watching the CEO of McDonalds pass up eating a Big Mac or Bill Gates avoiding Microsoft products. It tends to produce questioning concerning the produce or practice. Jesus graciously answers their question but not in a way that was expected. He does so by posing a question of his own in the form of analogy and then supports his question with two short parables.

Jesus' answer is complex and a little difficult to understand as it employs both imagery and metaphor that was common in his day but not so much today. We get most of our wine from the local bottle shop and tend to throw out old clothing. So the idea of sowing wineskins and darning clothes can be a little jarring to us. Jesus also used words such as new, old and the phrase 'in that day' which are chronologically open to interpretation. One person's 'old' might be another persons 'new' and so on. As a result it takes a little bit of digging to get to the treasure buried in these words of Jesus.

The first thing that we notice about this passage is that Jesus uses this questioning opportunity to make a clear statement about who he is. He is clearly saying to all around that he is the groom and that he is God. Jesus answers them by saying that nobody fasts in the presence of the groom when they are wedding guests. A few years ago I received an invitation for my cousins wedding. It was at the well-to-do end of town and in was a feast in every sense of the word. As timing would have it I was fasting about some really important issues leading up to the wedding. In fact I was on day 7 of a 40 day fast and I didn't want to disrupt the flow I had going. As I walked from the car to the venue I was very nervous. I was saying "God, help me, I want to keep fasting but don't want make a scene. What do I do?' In a moment of brilliance the

Holy Spirit reminded me not to be religious about fasting but rather get into the spirit of the feast tonight and then go back to fasting tomorrow. I was so grateful for this simple wisdom because it reminded me that in a time of feasting celebration there is no room to fast. The exact same thing Jesus was saying about his bodily presence.

The Old Testament prophets understood that God considered himself to be the husband of Israel. This can be seen in Isaiah 54:5, Ezekiel 16:10 and Hosea 2:16-20.[7] Jesus in answering this question from John's disciples used these very terms, which would have been familiar to the Pharisees, to say that He was God and he was in the presence of his wedding guests and that it was therefore a time for celebration. Other New Testament writers develop this theme further by painting the Church as the Bride. Ephesians 5:23 uses the analogy of a husband and wife being like Christ and the Church. 'As in oriental wedding custom, at the engagement (betrothal) the bride receives the promise of future blessing with her husband. Similarly, the church today is an espoused bride awaiting her husband's return from glory.'[8] Matthew 25:1-13 also employs the imagery of the bride waiting for the bridegroom to return.

Mark employs the term 'wedding guests' when referring to Jesus' disciples. This can leave the impression that Jesus was saying that a wedding was taking place at the point of which Jesus spoke. However, when we look at the description Matthew gives the disciples and the development of this theme in the New Testament we see that this wedding was one that was being anticipated in the future. Matthew refers to the disciples as nioi ton νυμφωνος meaning 'children of the bridechamber' or 'groomsmen'[9] and in so doing moves the meaning

---

7 Chatham, *Fasting: A Biblical Historical Study* 45.

8 P. Enns, *The Moody Handbook of Theology* (Chicago: Moody Press, 1989) 350

9 France, *Gospel of Mark: a commentary on the Greek text.* NIGTC 138.

from that of wedding guests at a wedding to 'friends of the bridegroom whose task it was to make the wedding arrangements'.[10] This is a really helpful way of understanding this term[11] as it reminds us of Revelation 19:6-9 which highlights the fact that 'the marriage supper of the Lamb' will take place as a final consummation of the Kingdom of God.[12]

In indentifying himself as the groom and the disciples as the groomsmen, Jesus backs up his new idea about fasting in The Sermon on the Mount by affirming that while Jesus is present it is not a time for fasting. In doing so Jesus confirms two things; firstly that fasting and mourning[13] were associated with each other as an expression of brokenness and desperation of sin or danger rather than just a commanded discipline. And secondly that Jesus' coming is too monumental to mark it with fasting because it was a great day. It was the long awaited fulfilment of Isaiah 62: 5.[14]

> *This is so stunning and so glorious and so unexpected in this form that Jesus said, you simply cannot fast now in this situation. It is too happy and too spectacularly exhilarating. Fasting is for times of yearning and aching and longing. But the Bridegroom of Israel is here. After a thousand years of dreaming and longing and hoping and waiting, he is here! The absence of fasting in the band of disciples was a witness to the presence of God in their midst.*[15]

---

10 Chatham, *Fasting: A Biblical Historical Study* 44.
11 R. A. Guelich, *Mark. Word Biblical commentary* (Dallas, Tex.: Word Books, 1989) 110.
12 Scobie, *The ways of our God* 792.
13 Calvin, *A harmony of the Gospels Matthew, Mark and Luke. Volume 1* 267.
14 Piper, *A Hunger for God: Desiring God through Fasting and Prayer* 35.
15 Piper, *A Hunger for God: Desiring God through Fasting and Prayer* 36.

It seems pretty clear that Jesus is saying that you simply cannot fast while I am present. It then beckons another question "will we ever fast again?" I would have been quite happy with Jesus if he had made it really clear that the whole deal was off. That for once and for all there would never again be a need to fast. I really enjoy food. I enjoy every flavour God has made except Asparagus. I enjoy every colour and texture of food and I love every cooking show known to man. I love steak that melts in your mouth and beans that snap in your teeth. Truth is I really love food. So why couldn't Jesus just declare it finished. Instead in verse 20 Jesus makes a statement about a time in which it will be appropriate for fasting again.

Jesus makes the cryptic statement that when the bridegroom is 'taken away from them' then they will fast again 'in that day'. The essential question now becomes what does 'In that day' mean? If I was to say to you that I'm coming around to your place "in that day" you would want to know which day I had in mind.

There are two major differing understandings of what Jesus is saying here about fasting. One group says that Jesus is 'taken away' on the day of his death and that his followers will mourn this single day.[16] The other way of thinking about this is that Jesus is 'taken away' at the ascension and then the church will be marked by fasting before the second coming.[17] There is a major interpretative difference between these two ideas. One group says that fasting finished with the first Easter and the other says that fasting continues throughout the church age. These words of Jesus and what they mean seem to be a really important pivotal point for a

---

16 P. Barnett, *The Servant King : reading Mark today*. (Sydney: Anglican Information Office, 1991) 55.

17 Piper, *A Hunger for God: Desiring God through Fasting and Prayer* 36.

theology of fasting and our understanding of how it works today.

The argument that Good Friday is what Jesus is referring to hangs on the point that in many places in the Old Testament that fasting has the function of mourning.[18] When you look at quite a few places in the Old Testament they would mourn and fast at the same time. So it is a fair enough link. The problem that arises with this line of thinking is when you replace one word for the other. In this line of thinking a major interpretative step is taken as the word 'fast' is replaced with 'mourn'. It turns Jesus words into a statement saying that he is predicting that the disciples will mourn on Good Friday. This is a very reasonable statement but doesn't seem to plumb the depths of what Jesus is teaching.

The major problem with this understanding is that mourning is not the only function of fasting in the Old Testament. It is a little bit like taking a word with a wide range of meanings and saying it has only one meaning. If I was to say to you that the word *watch* can only be understood as the timepiece that sits on your wrist, you would question me saying 'what about when you view something or when it is your turn to guard something or a warning to be careful'. And you would be right. It has a wide range of meanings. In the same way, the word *"fast"* has a wide range of functions in the Old Testament. It is not just about mourning.

It seems then that this first interpretation about the Mark 2 passage as being a day of sorrow flows from a narrow understanding[19] of the Old Testament function of fasting back into the New Testament text. Within this context some argue that John's disciples are fasting because they are

---

18 Calvin, *A harmony of the Gospels Matthew, Mark and Luke. Volume 1* 267. Lambert, *Fasting* in Sakenfeld, (Ed) *The New Interpreter's dictionary of the Bible* 431.

19 Garland, *Mark in Zondervan Illustrated Bible backgrounds commentary* 222.

mourning his death. Again this is very narrow and not explicit in the text. Cranfield says that it is likely that John's disciples fasted during his life as well.[20] Another point is that even though the disciples did mourn the crucifixion there is nothing indicating that they fasted during these few days.[21] One would think that if Mark's thrust here was to make a statement that the ultimate and final fast was soon upon the disciples then he would have made it explicit that the disciples fasted over the first Easter. Rather, none of the Gospel writers comment on an Easter fast, therefore making this understanding unlikely.

The phrase 'but the days will come' is used in Luke's Gospel to announce an eschatological event. That is, an event that is yet to come but is not really linked to a particular calendar date so much as a period of time. In Luke 17:22 it is used in reference to the coming of the Kingdom and in 21:6 to the future destruction of Jerusalem.[22] In fact in Luke's account of this same passage in Mark 2 he opts for the plural 'in those days'. 'Obviously, Matthew and Luke took Mark's "on that day" as being synonymous with "the days will come" that begin the verse'.[23] By using this phrase ἐκείνῃ τῇ ἡμέρᾳ Mark infers that a future eschatological time period is being referred to rather than a day or two. [24] It is an excessive literalism to take this phrase as meaning the day of Jesus' death only. 'The reference is more generally to a coming time when the immediate excitement of Jesus' ministry will give way to a more settled style of

---

20 C.E.B. Cranfield, *The Gospel according to Saint Mark* (Cambridge, Eng.: Cambridge University Press, 1959) 108.

21 D. Lachman, and F. J. Smith, (Eds) *Worship in the Presence of God* (Greenville, S.C.: Greenville Seminary Press, 1992) 267.

22 Guelich, *Mark. Word Biblical commentary* 110.

23 Guelich, *Mark. Word Biblical commentary* 112.

24 France, *Gospel of Mark: a commentary on the Greek text.* NIGTC 140.

discipleship in which fasting will take its proper place'.[25]

In the years following the disciples probably did not understand Jesus being 'taken away' as the crucifixion as they spent time with him after the resurrection.

> *Jesus can be understood to have rejected only the mourning custom of fasting (Matt 9:15) and not all other kinds...certainly, his church could not have understood fasting as a mourning custom for removal of the bridegroom, for the Risen Christ was still continually present with the community.*[26]

Luke in Acts 1:3 describes Jesus appearing and teaching them many times between the resurrection and his ascension. Luke also refers to the ascension as Jesus being 'taken up'. This idea of Jesus being taken up and Mark's idea of *taken away* seem to indicate that the ascension is what Jesus has in mind as he talks about the right time to fast again.

It can be really hard to work out how the disciples understood what Jesus was saying but equally vital in gaining a correct understanding. The modern reader wasn't present so we look for clues about how those who heard him in the flesh understood his words. This is going to be a really critical point. If the disciples never fast again then we can take it that what Jesus really meant was that fasting is finished. So whether the early church continued to fast or not gives us an important insight as to how they understood this text. If they had understood fasting as finishing at the Resurrection then there probably would have been no fasting mentioned again except if the narrative was describing Yom Kippur being adhered to by the Jews. Instead we are presented with a history changing missional decision in Acts 13 that has its genesis in

---

[25] France, *Gospel of Mark: a commentary on the Greek text.* NIGTC 140.
[26] Muddiman, *Fasting* in D. N. Freedman, *The Anchor Bible dictionary* 775.

the prophets fasting to worship and seek God.[27] We see the prophets and teachers of the New Testament church fasting. This is really key. It means they, the ones closest to Jesus, took Jesus' words to mean that *in that day* had started. This is no leftover religious practice that they had not been able to kick. It is something that is Holy Spirit induced and had fire and encounter all over it.

In contrast with this understanding of Mark's text some *Form critics* say that verses 19b-20 was an addition by the early church scribes to modify what Jesus was saying to conform to the practice of fasting in the Church.[28] That is, the church had a habit of Old Testament fasting that they couldn't get free from so they altered the text to justify their left over practice. What is a *Form critic* you say? It is a type of Bible scholars who read the text and says there is no way this could have been what happened. So they try to work out who added what afterwards. So their premise is that the church kept fasting out of a religious practice and then went back and modified Jesus' words in Mark's gospel and these modifications are what we have today.

These *Form critics* argue that this Mark 2 passage is a Passion prediction that is too early within the gospel. The worldview they are operating from is that the word of God is not really the word of God just rather a bunch of ideas from man. They say that Jesus didn't really know that he was going to die in the way he did early in his ministry. The form critics also point out a supposed change of tone towards fasting as presented between 19a and verse 20.[29] So the big idea these critics have is that the early church couldn't shake the idea of holding a religious fast because

---

27 Piper, *A Hunger for God: Desiring God through Fasting and Prayer* 36.

28 Muddiman, *Fasting* in Freedman, *The Anchor Bible dictionary* 776.

29 Cranfield, *The Gospel according to Saint Mark* 111.

they had been used to doing it as Jews, so they kept doing it and made it Christian in tone and language.

At this point I hope I haven't lost you. Are for following this thread? This is a really important point that I don't want you to miss. It's a little heavy going but is vital to understand. The point is that some say the fasting the church did was a Jewish habit that they couldn't break so they renamed it and dressed it up Christian. A bit like the little habits we have. We get into a flow and then can't stop. The truth about this was that the church was caught praying, worshiping and fasting in Acts 13 in a completely non-religious way. It wasn't a habit they were just performing without thinking but a response to Jesus' words in Mark 2 saying the period of time was here.

In response to these Form critics it must be noted that there exists no evident that the early church conducted some type of memorial fast that they wanted to justify by addition to the original text.[30] Did you get that? No evidence exists anywhere that the church kept fasting according to a Jewish tradition. There was no need for them to alter the text because they had nothing to justify. Likewise, in terms of Passion, Jesus at his baptism understood that the language of the suffering servant in Isaiah applied to his mission. So there is no sense that this Passion prediction is too early.[31] In reality Jesus knew all along why he came. It is only those who read the bible with a carnal mind that miss this.

In the same way, there only seems to be internal conflict within the passage if you interpret the passage to be saying that fasting is ending once and for all rather than suspended while the Groom is present. That is, the passage reads really consistently if you interpret it well. Jesus is

---

30 Muddiman, *Fasting* in Freedman, *The Anchor Bible dictionary* 776.

31 Cranfield, *The Gospel according to Saint Mark* 111.

saying not now but really soon. My kids ask me all the time for things that it is not quite time for. They would love to have a chocolate biscuit before dinner. I really want them to have one. They taste awesome. However I don't want them to eat it before dinner as it makes dinner taste not as great and might fill them up a bit. So I say later. My answer becomes not a yes or no but rather, first you have to do this and then it is the right time. There is nothing inconsistent about this. It is all about timing. Like I said a few pages back…timing is everything.

The poetic structure of this passage yields some important clues as well. There is a use of parallelism between 19a and 19b that is key. Jesus is saying the same thing in two different ways. The first asks a question and the second as the answer to that question. The parallelism is Jesus' way of adding emphasis. It's like he cups his hands around his mouth to speak with extra volume. "Can you fast with the Groom here? Of course you can't!" This helps us to see that the text is a unified whole and should not be understood as non-original.[32] Therefore we should approach it as a unified whole straight from the heart of God. Not picking the bits we like and leaving the rest.[33]

The second half of this passage in Mark 2 is concerned with two parables about what Jesus has just been speaking on. One parable is concerning cloth and the other wine but both seem to be presenting a case of incompatibility between the new and the old.[34] This makes total sense. The new and the old don't mix. The question for many becomes what is the old and the new that Jesus is talking about. I've heard preachers say that Jesus is talking about new models for ministry

---

32 Cranfield, *The Gospel according to Saint Mark* 111.

33 Muddiman, *Fasting* in Freedman, *The Anchor Bible dictionary* 776.

34 R. H. Gundry, *A Survey of the New Testament* (Grand Rapids USA; Zondervan, 1981) 129.

or new methods of doing things. It seems to be a verse that is trotted out for anybody who wants to justify a new way to do anything. All these applications may well be right and useful and spirit lead but we can't afford to simply jump over the very topic Jesus is teaching about; fasting. We need to understand these parables in there context first.

Some say that Jesus has moved on to a new topic. He has dealt with fasting and now is moving on. The New Testament scholar France notes that there is no syntactic link between the parables and the discussion of fasting.[35] That is, Jesus doesn't use the word fast or groom or wedding again so he must have moved on to a new topic. While this may seem possible, in a literary sense we have demonstrated that as opposed to the view of the Form critics this passage is a unitary whole.[36] It is best understood as one work or a whole making a united point. We have also observed the use of the word *fast* 6 times in verses 18-20. It would seem likely from this that Jesus is using the two parables to illustrate what he has been saying about the role of fasting. That would make sense from a context point of view. The sticky point we have in declaring this outright is the use of the phrases *new wine* and *old wine*.

The interpretation of what old wine and new wine mean can be a bit tricky. Some scholars highlight a macro view. That is, they take a big picture approach and say that Jesus moves from the direct issue in front of him and widens it to include all aspects of his now dawning Kingdom. Some other scholars highlight the micro. That is, Jesus is only concerned for one issue right now. On the macro level some scholars such

---

35 France, *Gospel of Mark: a commentary on the Greek text*. NIGTC 137.
36 Piper, *A Hunger for God: Desiring God through Fasting and Prayer* 38.

as Gundry[37], Bock[38] and Rothenberg[39] highlight the view that Jesus tells the parable to illustrate a point that the new kingdom is coming and it not comparable with the old. These scholars are thinking big picture and see it pointing to Jesus as the new wine and the Kingdom of God as the new wineskin. While there is little doubt amongst conservative scholars[40] as to this point Piper highlights the micro as well without rejecting the macro. Piper says that because of the context of the discussion of fasting, you can't escape the reality that the old wineskin is a reference to the old style of Jewish fasting and that the new kingdom will have a new wine, that is radical New Testament fasting. This new fasting is divorced from mourning over sin and is centred on the triumph of God and longs for the consummation of the Kingdom.[41]

So a new invitation has been issued. Not to a feast yet but a fast. And

---

37 Gundry, *A Survey of the New Testament* 129.
38 D. L. Bock, *Gospel of Luke* in D. G. Reid (Ed), *The IVP Dictionary of the New Testament* (Illinois USA.: IVP, 2004) 766.
39 Rothenberg, *Fast* in Brown (Ed) *The new international dictionary of New Testament theology*.
40 In the modern era there has arisen some questions about the traditional interpretation of this double parable as being about incompatibility. It is argued that Luke adds verse 39 of his account which dramatically changes the meaning of the double parable. Luke adds 'and no one after drinking old wine desires new, for he says "the old is good"'. Lancaster states that in the context of Jesus choosing his disciples, Luke is making a comment that new disciples are needed for the new wine of the kingdom. His interpretation is based on Avot 4 and states the meaning of the parable as saying Jesus needed previously uneducated students in order to receive what Jesus is giving. The downfall of this compatibility theory is that it takes the addition of Luke as Jesus making a factual editorial comment rather than Jesus reporting the current view amongst the Jews at his time that they wouldn't accept the new because the old appeals to the human desire to atone for oneself. D. T. Lancaster *New Wine and Old Wineskins: The Parable of Luke 5:36-39 Re-examined* (http://www.bethimmanuel.org/) accessed on 23/10/2008
41 Piper, *A Hunger for God: Desiring God through Fasting and Prayer* 38.

not to a fast of the past but a new type of fasting. A fasting that changes history and breaks the fear of man off. A fasting that prepares you to host the presence of the Holy Spirit in powerful ways. A type of fasting that causes bridal intimacy and enables the Holy Spirit's whispers to be heard over the deafening sounds of life. The critical question is will you respond to such an invitation and break the trends of a generation?

# 3.

# INVITATION TO EMPOWERMENT

There is no doubt in my mind that I need more of the Holy Spirit's power on my life for what lies ahead. There is so much work to do in seeing the Kingdom manifested on earth as it is in Heaven that I am convinced I need more power. My life context screams that I need more power. My wife Kate and I and our four kids moved ten years ago from our comfortable country house to the busiest and most densely populated part of our nation. We lived in Bondi Junction in Sydney's Eastern suburbs and planted a church there called The Hope Project. It was the result of an encounter with the Holy Spirit one morning as I was facedown on the carpet. We came from a location in which the town of 40 000 people had about 36 churches to choose from. That's about a church for every 1000 people. We came to a place in which within a 2km radius of the heart of Bondi Junction about 65 000 people live and within that space there was about 3 churches. I'll do the maths for you. That's about one church per 22 000 people. And I'm not talking about big churches here. Think 100 or less on average. This is a place, according to a Pastor friend of mine, where over the last 10 years or so 20 church plants have started and only two survived. This is a place in with the Australian Bureau of Statistics say that it is about 2 to 3% Christian.

This is a place where the young and hip come to get noticed and the up and coming professional dwell. It is a place which is desperately needy for an outpouring of God.

And what does this outpouring look like. It looks like me. Jesus sent me. Out of all the people Jesus could have tapped on the shoulder, he tapped me. So as I stood at my high-rise window or in the Oxford st Mall or as I walked down Bondi Rd past all the hip café's, I cried out to God. My prayer was simple. "Release your power Lord, on this place." I need more power. I've only prayed for a few and seen God's healing power released. Most we talk to about Jesus say that it's nice for us but they are at a different place. I need more power so I can continue Jesus' mission of proclaiming the good news to all, setting the captives free, recovering sight to the blind, bringing liberty to the oppressed, destroying the works of the evil ones, displaying the abundant life and making sure that everybody on my turf gets at least one opportunity to here the Gospel with the demonstration of the Spirit's power in such a way that their heart is gripped. Yes my friend I need more power.

I would imagine that you need more power as well. You might be facing the mundane or the extraordinary. You might be facing the clothes washing or the next step in ministry. Either way, whatever you are facing, I imagine you need God's power to do it well. You need a breakthrough of the Spirit's power to do what needs to be done. It doesn't matter if the realm is work, family, business, pastoral or relational. We all need a breakthrough. Fasting is that invitation to have more of the Spirit's power operating in your life. The bible shows us two clear times in which this new type of fasting is linked to hosting a greater degree of the Spirit's power. If you are ready for increased power in your life then read on.

## Jesus' forty day Fast

The impact of hearing that the Spirit of God led Jesus into the wilderness to fast for forty days is a little lost on modern readers. We just read over it quickly and it doesn't really jar us. I often read the bible text way too fast and miss the buried treasure. This is partly because we mostly know what happens next in the narrative and partly because forty days of the timeline of the story are expressed in a very short passage of time. However, the idea of Jesus fasting is really quite shocking. Think about it for a minute. What on earth was he doing? It's also clear that it wasn't some sort of habit or tradition or something that was expected because Luke makes it really clear that The Holy Spirit led him. And this comes after an incredible announcement that Jesus was here to do business. As far as Jesus' ministry it was now all systems go. However, he stops, breaks momentum and disappears into the desert. So the question remains; what was Jesus doing out there?

Fasting in the Old Testament was associated with, amongst other things, sin that needed to be atoned for, mourning and repentance.[42] But we understand that Jesus had no sin of his own to atone for. He was perfectly God. There was no need for mourning and no need for repentance. So we can't understand this fast as a function of the Old Testament mourning and repentance. So what was he doing?

Luke goes to great lengths in his gospel to portray Jesus as very much the opposite of John's ascetic lifestyle.[43] That is Luke emphasises Jesus being one who was with the people and at the parties. He is not shown as one who was always out in the wilderness and trying to constantly deny

---

[42] J. Piper, *A Hunger for God: Desiring God through Fasting and Prayer* (USA: Crossway Books, 1997) 35.

[43] Piper, *A Hunger for God: Desiring God through Fasting and Prayer* 34.

the flesh. This was not Jesus' default place according to Luke. So what was he doing out there?

All three synoptic gospels describe this event of Jesus being in the wilderness but with quite a different emphasise. Matthew in 4:1-11 makes the focus of the narrative, the actual temptations that Jesus experiences, by starting the phrase with the purpose clause 'to be tempted by the devil'. So, according to Matthew, Jesus went into the wilderness so that he would have a power encounter with the devil and withstand him. Mark includes the story in Mark 1: 12-13 but does not mention the fasting or the nature of the temptations. This is quite typical of Mark's emphasis[44] to move the narrative along quickly so as to focus on the ministry of Jesus. Luke however adds a narrative frame that Matthew does not. This is a really important commentary by Luke. He doesn't just give us the events but he adds something to the beginning and end of the passage to gain our attention. A bit like a narrator saying *don't miss this bit, it's the best bit*. Luke in 4:1 starts with the phrase 'Jesus, full of the Holy Spirit' and finishes the story with the phrase in 4:14 'Jesus returned in the power of the Spirit'. This phrase is often[45] used by Luke, as a favourite expression for a character that is truly of God.[46] This comment by Luke shows a difference in Jesus between the going in and the coming out. The Spirit had just descended on Jesus before this episode but now Jesus was returning with the power. Something had happened to Jesus during this fast and now he was ready to show his power. This phrase by Luke really showed that 'his ministry, like the church's later ministry, was

---

44 In the same way Mark doesn't include any genealogy or infancy narratives.

45 13 times in Luke-Acts

46 R. H. Stein. *Luke. NAC* (Nashville, Tenn.: Broadman Press, 1992) 145.

marked by the Spirit's power'.[47]

So while there is a clear linking by Luke to the endowment of power there still remains other questions as to why Jesus fasted for 40 days in the wilderness. There seems to be three schools of thought that attempt to answer this question. The first school is that Jesus was symbolising Israel's experience in the wilderness for 40 years but with a different outcome. The second school of thought is that Jesus was prepared for his ministry through the trial of fasting and the third is similar to the second in that it talks about Jesus' preparation as a model for the life of Christian discipleship for the disciples and beyond.

There is no escaping that Luke uses elements of the 40 years of wilderness wanderings by Israel to frame the wilderness experience of Jesus for 40 days. There is the element of divine leading, the use of the '40'[48] motif and the location being the wilderness.[49] This passage also parallels Deuteronomy 8: 2-3 to show that the Old Testament shadow is replaced with the New Testament reality. Luke portrays Jesus as the fulfilment of Deuteronomy 18: 15, that is, a new prophetic deliverer to take the people of God into the metaphorical Promised Land.[50] Jesus is also directly linked to Moses by the fact that they both fasted for 40 days.[51] 'The success of Jesus in the wilderness recalls Israel's failure there. Jesus is qualified to lead the nation, and his success gives promise

---

47 Stein. *Luke. NAC* 148

48 J. Nolland, *Luke 1 - 9:20.Word Biblical Commentary* (Dallas, Tex.: Word Books, 1989) 178.

49 J. B. Green, *The Gospel of Luke. NICNT* (Grand Rapids, Mich.: William B. Eerdmans, 1997) 192.

50 Piper, *A Hunger for God: Desiring God through Fasting and Prayer* 55-57.

51 G. H. Twelftree, *Temptation of Jesus* in .J. B. Green and S. McKnight, (Eds) *Dictionary of Jesus and the Gospels* (Downers Grove, Ill.: IVP, 1992) 824.

of ultimate success against all spiritual enemies'.[52]

Luke uses this passage to demonstrate that Israel has a new deliverer who is empowered by the Holy Spirit. However, to say that this passage is simply symbolic misses out on something. This passage also functions not just as symbol showing the new king but also actually in preparing Jesus for the earthly ministry. That is, Jesus didn't only fast to fulfil a shadow of the Old Testament but the fast actually did something to prepare him for that kingly role. If our Christological focus at this point is on the divinity of Christ we may have problems with this fast functioning in this way because Christ was perfectly God. However, we must also remember that He was fully man and as such needed to have his human side kept in check. In this way the fast and the temptations also function as the last preparatory episode before his public ministry.[53]

Tertullian, a prolific early Christian author from Carthage, draws a parallel with 1 Samuel 7:6 and comments that not only was Jesus' forty day fast about preparation for ministry but also for war with Satan.[54] The victory that Christ has over the flesh and over Satan is established firmly within this episode of fasting. 'Jesus began his ministry with fasting. And he triumphed over his enemy with fasting. And our salvation was accomplished through perseverance by fasting'.[55]

The logical extension from this thought is; that the fast of Jesus was not just symbol or fulfilling shadow but actually preparatory in overcoming Satan and the flesh. Therefore it is a valid model for his disciples, not just then but for all time, in their preparation for ministry and the endowment

---

[52] D. L. Bock, *Luke. Volume 1. 1:1 - 9:50.* (Grand Rapids, Mich. Baker Books, 1994).

[53] Stein. *Luke. NAC* 144.

[54] Smith-Christopher, *Fasting* in Freedman, & Myers, (Ed) *Eerdmans dictionary of the Bible* 456.

[55] Piper, *A Hunger for God: Desiring God through Fasting and Prayer* 55.

of power that is needed for that ministry to be effective.

This idea of empowerment has been developed in differing ways over the years of the history of the church. Some disciples have fasted for forty days, some for smaller periods, while the church developed the 40 day Lenten fast before Easter to partake in this discipline. Twelftree argues that Matthew understands the fast of Jesus as setting a model by which his disciples would follow because his gospel is the only one to give disciples directions on how to fast a little while later at the Sermon on the Mount.[56] So its entirely possible that as Matthew wrote his gospel, as he decides which passages of Jesus' life to include and which ones to exclude, he knew readers would assume fasting was for them so he makes sure to include Jesus' words about how to do it well and not become religious about it in Matthew 6: 16-18. Another scholar, Merrill, points out that there could be no other expectation other than that the disciples would model what Jesus has done. 'The fact that Jesus and the disciples sanctioned it by their own example (Matt 4:2, Acts 13:2-3) however is sufficient justification for it's practice in biblical times and in fact, in modern times as well'.[57]

At this point it is really important to talk about the different between description and prescription. If I was watching somebody tightrope across Niagara Falls I would have no sense that there was an implied invitation for me to do the same and follow suit. I would be very happy to watch and describe it but to stay with my feet on solid ground. The difficulty with Jesus' life is that he often said "come follow me and do the works I do". However, it could be pointed out that Jesus died by

---

[56] Twelftree, *Temptation of Jesus* in Green and McKnight, (Eds) *Dictionary of Jesus and the Gospels* 825.

[57] Merrill,. *Fasting* in Elwell, *Evangelical dictionary of theology* 245.

crucifixion and there is clearly no expectation that we follow suit in a literal way. That would put a whole new twist on the WWJD bracelet movement. What we have to work out is what parts of his life were all about watching (description) and which ones were all about following and doing the same (prescription).

It seems to me that outside of the clear invitations of Jesus to follow and do like wise, the function of any action must also be considered when determining which actions he meant for us to model and which ones did he mean for us not to emulate. The function of the crucifixion was to pay the perfect sacrifice for the sin of the world. The function of this action rules out any modelling or copying as we cannot and do not need to perform that function. It was done once and for all and needs no attempt at a copy by a fallen human. However, Jesus did many other actions that were meant to be copied; he prayed, he cared, set the oppressed free, he spoke out for God and against injustice, healed the sick and destroyed the works of the evil one. The function of all of these activities, that is, seeing the Kingdom come to earth as it is in Heaven, would indicate that not only were the actions valid for the specific moment Jesus did them but also for those who would come after him. Jesus was the example of how to live for God and he is to be copied in many ways. After all Jesus said in John 14: 12 that those who believe in Jesus will do even greater works than what he did. So the function of being Jesus' ambassadors on earth dictates that we do the works Jesus did except those that were specifically for him alone to carry out.

John Calvin however sharply disagrees with the notion that Jesus' forty day fast is a model in any way. He argues that Christ's fast was not about temperance but rather to show himself more divine than the common man.[58] He says that it is foolishness for the prophets and the

---

58 Calvin, *A harmony of the Gospels Matthew, Mark and Luke. Volume 1* 134.

Fathers to imitate Moses. However, the context of Calvin very much shapes his opinion. He was confronted in the Renaissance Age with a Catholic church that had turned the fast of Christ into a model, which was Lent, and then allowed it to become an enforced ritual that had over time lost meaning and become a good work to attain holiness. People on the Lenten fast would "stuff themselves" before breakfast and then "fast" all day. For many it had become a religious event rather than a genuine seeking after God. It had become about outward form and not heart connection with Jesus, and it was religious form this that Calvin rallied against. The point being that any good and Godly thing can be overtaken by the religious spirit if we do it just because we always have.

This type of fasting appalled Calvin and he spoke out against this gross form of modelling. However, Calvin was not against all fasting, just this type; 'now I am not speaking of fasting in general, for I would wish its use (as long as it is sound) could be more frequent amongst us, but I had to show the aim of the fast of Christ'.[59] John Calvin believed that fasting is good if it increases our desire for prayer and testifies to the trueness of our repentance.[60] So arguably Calvin's greatest reason for rejecting the fast of Christ as a model was the way it was being conducted by the Catholic Church rather than the concept of fasting itself.

At this point it might help to add some of my own experience because I have had a few conversations about this very idea over the last decade. Sometimes people will say to me the idea of fasting for more than a few hours is pure foolishness because the human body cannot go without food for more than a few days. I wondered the same before my first 40 day fast. I had had it said to me that I would die. However as I read more about it from a health and medical perspective I was surprised. A

---

59 Calvin, *A harmony of the Gospels Matthew, Mark and Luke. Volume 1* 135.
60 Calvin, *A harmony of the Gospels Matthew, Mark and Luke. Volume 1* 215.

secular article I read told the story of a man who wished to kill himself via fasting after his wife had left him. The story goes that he headed for the hills to do just that. After something like 60 or 70 days he came to his senses and realised life was worth holding on to. He came down the mountain and continued with his life. The point being, that he was mentally functioning better at the end rather than the start of the fast and it had increased his cognitive functioning.

I was encouraged by this information when I started my first 40 day fast. Mostly the fasting I do is juice fasting. That is during the day I will sip on juice. Mostly because I don't have the luxury of going into a wilderness experience and resting all day. Like most people, work and family are necessary to maintain. So I would have juice. Not too much and not too little. Just enough to get by. The main thing I discovered is that you can go a lot longer than you think without food. We have become a society that has bought into the lie that is pushed by some food manufacturers that you must have food on hand all day and eat multiple times a day. The truth however is that you don't really need to. You can go a few hours or even days if you really want to. My experience over the last decade is that if you plan carefully most people can do a three day fast and quite a few people I know have not only done one 40 day but multiple fasts. So it seems that Jesus was doing something in a 40 day fast that others could do as well.

So it seems entirely possible then that the 40 fast of Jesus functioned on a couple of levels. Yes it was a symbol of his superiority to Israel but it also allowed the power of the Holy Spirit to empower him in the context of resisting the temptation of the devil. In this context we see it as a model of a fasted life. The call might not be for 40 days straight but a lifestyle in which it is part of the regular seasons of life.

## Only by Prayer and Fasting

Jesus is not finished with the idea of linking empowerment of the Holy Spirit and fasting. So far it has been about his example of the 40 day fast and how Luke frames that, but now we move to the very words of Jesus. We find in Mark's gospel a power encounter in which the disciples are not able to bring deliverance to a possessed child. The story is in Mark 9:14-29 and tells of a boy with a deaf and dumb spirit. The narrative picks up a scene in which the disciples have tried to set him free but have failed. Jesus is called in to help and a bystander says that the disciples were asked to set him free but they were unable to.

At first glance this is a puzzling situation as we have seen a few chapters earlier Jesus give these same disciples authority over every unclean spirit. Jesus had expressly set them up for these types of situations. They had been given all they needed. We know from Luke and Matthew that they exercised this authority very effectively as well. So the passage in Mark is designed to jar us. It's designed to make us stop in our tracks and ask about what has happened to this power that the disciples were used to. So we have some people with the authority to heal and deliver - but they were unable to. Mark is setting us up to ask the question "what is it going to take to see this boy delivered?"

The first thing we notice is that Jesus is not really impressed about the situation. He fully expects that at this stage of the development of the disciples they would know what to do. An interesting side note on this point is that the standard answer as to why Jesus can and would heal and other humans sometimes fail is that Jesus was the Son of God and we are not. The expectation is that we are mere humans so we shouldn't expect to use such power. Jesus however sets up no false dichotomy here at all. You don't see Jesus saying "I'm God and you are not so don't expect to do powerful things." In fact we are confronted with the very opposite.

Jesus is frustrated by the disciples not being able. He fully expects that they should be able to. He says "O, Faithless generation, how long am I to be with you? How long am I to bear with you? Bring him to me". Jesus healing this boy is plan B. His plan A was that by this stage the disciples would know what to do and how to exercise the authority needed.

This sets up a dramatic conclusion to the drama. The disciples ask the question that is on the readers lips. Why was Jesus able to do that and the disciples not? It is interesting that Jesus' answer was not that they didn't have enough faith. In his frustration beforehand Jesus says *faithless generation* so one might expect him to say it was a lack of faith. It is almost like he is making a comment about their development rather than their faith. After all, they attempted to deliver the boy. They had delivered many before that as well. They had no reason to doubt that they would set this boy free. It was the first time it *hadn't worked* so it seems unlikely that faith was the issue.

Jesus simply says that you couldn't deliver the child because this type of spiritual guest only comes out via prayer and fasting. That was probably not the explanation that they were expecting. For Mark this answer acts like a punch line at the climax of a story. It is meant to shock us. It is meant to mess with our minds and make us think, "hold on that can't be right". Even more incredible is that Jesus doesn't stop to pray and fast before he attempts deliverance. He doesn't even pray for the Father to deliver the boy. He instead addresses the spirit and commands him to come out. So what is really going on here? At no point in the story does Jesus pray or fast yet he says that the answer is in praying and fasting.

The fact that Jesus doesn't stop at that moment to pray and fast is also part of the answer. It forces us to think that Jesus might not be talking about momentary prayers but rather lifestyle. If Jesus had said at this injunction that he was calling a 3 day fast and then he would come back and then he would pray, we could then pretty safely interpret his answer to mean that as the need arises we should pray and fast. Instead he doesn't do that and we are forced to think beyond the moment to that of habits and lifestyle. <u>Jesus is inferring that a lifestyle of prayer and fasting is the key to greater moments of power and breakthrough.</u> I wonder whether this is part of his frustration with the disciples. We know in other places such as Luke 11 they ask Jesus to teach them to pray and that at the Garden of Gethsemane they couldn't pray for an hour. Jesus is spelling out the path to empowerment through the lifestyle of prayer and fasting not just responding to crisis with momentary prayer and fasting.

Some versions of the Bible leave us with Mark 9: 29 as saying just prayer and not fasting. Often in the footnotes it will say something about some manuscripts adding the word fasting. When the passage is rendered this way it puts a psychological question mark over the importance of the word that is being added. It makes us feel like somebody has come along later and added something. It is just as valid to render it with the word fasting included and add the note *some manuscripts only have prayer*. The reality is for this passage many ancient manuscripts have the word fasting and only some don't. So the team that put a translation of the Bible together have to make a decision; to include the word or not. Those committees entrusted with the decision for their version, who leave it out say that it was probably added by ascetics later on to justify their practice of fasting. Their idea being that the ascetic community fasted so much that they needed to justify this from scripture so as they hand copied the text they started to add *and fasting*.

Many people today would never consider adding to or taking away from scripture. We understand it as God's inspired word. We study hard to make sure we are saying what it is saying. So why do we not make the same assumptions of those who lovingly and painstaking hand copied every single copy so you and I could have it today. So we are left with two ways to think about how the text came to be as it is. Either a majority of scribing groups added to the text or a minority deleted from the text. Adding to the text would appear to be deliberate whereas taking away from the text could be either deliberate or a mistake made in a few geographical locations. It seems more reasonable to assume the best from the skilled scribes and say that the original was *prayer and fasting* and that a minority of scribes made a mistake when coping and deleted *and fasting*.

Those who disagree with including fasting in this text point to the major important original texts as not having the word fasting. Whereas, those who advocate include the word fasting say that the majority of ancient texts include fasting. At this point it can become is a bit of a subjective issue as we can't really be sure. So we look for hints that might help us unlock the puzzle and point us one way or the other. However, when you trace a well developed theology of fasting and how Jesus develops the thinking around fasting, it seems to me a completely consistent approach include the word fasting in this text and understand fasting as a source of Holy Spirit empowerment.

## Physical Exhaustion

The irony of all this talk about fasting being linked to empowerment of the Holy Spirit is that while fasting you can feel incredibly physically weak. There have been many times while fasting in which I just can't do the task required of me. Or I end up doing it a lot slower than I would have hoped for. It means the normal way you receive power through food is cut off. No only does your body feel slow and lethargic but your brain is not as sharp at times as well. This may seem like a contradiction to the story in which the man who fasted for 70 day became cognitively sharper but the reality is that you experience many times of physical exhaustion during fasting as well as moments of incredible mental clarity. Fasting leaves you in a heightened state of understanding the importance of food and its function to keep you able. The tasks that are normally easy to you can become hard.

But even this physical weakness is part of the glory of fasting. It forms a powerful metaphor for the way God works through human beings. Paul spoke in 2 Corinthians 10 about power and weakness. While the primary context probably isn't fasting it certainly is a fitting metaphor for what happens when we fast. It says in verses 9 and 10

> *My grace is sufficient for you, for my power is made perfect in weakness. Therefore I will boast all the more gladly of my weaknesses, so that the power of Christ may rest upon me. For the sake of Christ, then, I am content with weaknesses, insults, hardships, persecutions, and calamities. For when I am weak, then I am strong.*

The overall emphasis of what Paul is saying is that while we are weak as humans the power of God can flow through us. Weakness makes as prime candidates for the explosion of God's infinite power.

It is not very much of a stretch to apply this passage to the context of fasting. It is fitting in terms of God's power filling the void of human weakness. It also fits well within Pauline theology as fasting was something that Paul did regularly. There are two passages in which Paul is being quite autobiographical. In these passages he tells us some of the things he would do and some of the things done to him. The most telling of these two passages is 2 Corinthians 11:27. It is a list of some of the things he has endured as an apostle. The ESV reads very strangely. It reads *in toil and hardship, through many a sleepless night, in hunger and thirst, often without food, in cold and exposure.* The interesting thing about the ESV is that it doubles up on the idea of going without food and tries to make it sound like going without was something done to Paul. What is eye opening is when you go to the Greek and see that the ESV translators have made a decision to avoid the word "fasting" even though it is clearly there and makes the verse easier to understand. The Greek word for fasting is νηστείαις (nēsteiais) and is clearly what Paul had in mind rather than just going without food. The word hunger is a different word λιμῷ (limō). The correct understanding of the verse according to the Greek is that Paul experienced times of hunger and thirst in the passive sense but that he also often fasted. The idea that Paul is trying to communicate is that he was subjected to hunger but he often subjected himself to fastings. This is also backed up by the passage in 2 Corinthians 6: 5 as well. It uses the word fasting as something that Paul has experienced even thought most modern versions opt for the word hunger. The difference is critical. Hunger is all about not having access to food but fasting is all about going with out food in order to pray and seek God.

This is no small point. It helps us understand the mindset of Paul. It helps us see that when he spoke about weakness he really knew what he was talking about. He knew what it was to subject himself to fasting in order that he would see the power of God. The passage also helps us to see that fasting was not a one off event for Paul, but rather it was part of his spiritual rhythms of life. The adverb which accompanies the noun "fasting" is "often". Paul wants us to see that part of his normal spiritual rhythm was to fast. So when Paul talks about weakness of the flesh, we are hearing from somebody who fasted regularly. It leaves little doubt that when Paul spoke of fasting he had the physical aspect of weakness in mind. This regular fasting of Paul adds strength to the idea that the early church understood Jesus' words in Mark 2 to mean that the church age would be the age of fasting.

So the invitation has been issued. The reality is that so many settle for a powerless Christian walk and then build a theology around that. Jesus' intention is that we would be filled with the power of the Holy Spirit and this power would overflow. His intention was that we would find that quiet place of prayer and fasting where this power is renewed. But so often we are so busy and so consumed with our own ability and with the desire for food and the comfort that it brings. The Holy invitation is being issued to you. It has been issued to the church. It has been issued to the Bride. To leave self behind, fuel ministry and life, and find real power. Make the decision today to RSVP to this invitation and find a renewing power like none other. Respond today to the invitation to a fast. It's never too late to respond.

# 4.

# INVITATION TO CHANGE HISTORY

There is not a single human being alive who does not see something in their life or the world around them and long for the ability to go back and change history. It might be a foolish decision made while younger or some of the man-made tragedies on a global scale. Whatever the context we wish we could wind back the clock and do some things differently. We wish we could change history. Mostly because the present reality and outworking of the past is sometimes too hard to bear.

It is a bit of a strange concept that of changing history. In its most literal sense there is no going back like *Back to the Future* and changing events. There are no time machines and no way to alter the actual events of history either on a personal or corporate sense. But there is a way of altering the natural and logical consequences of those past moments. In the same way there is always the possibility to write a new present and future history. Really what we are saying by using the term changing history is that history appears to be panning out one way and we desire it to take a different path. What we are really talking about is presenting a society or family line that is different to the current trajectory. In this way we can function as, as Lou Engle terms it, the *Hinge of History*. That moment when a new path is taken that is radically different to the past.

In the personal sense it is like the day that a person gets saved, or filled with the Spirit or set free from some vice. It is a day that they will look back upon and say that their whole history changed. It was the hinge of history for them. In the same way we all have cultural and social hinges that we look back upon and say something shifted there. I think back to the Great Awakenings with the likes of Jonathan Edwards. In the 1973 sermon entitled "The Role Of Prayer In Spiritual Awakening" by Dr J. Edwin Orr, he describes an era before the Great Awakening in which it was commonly thought that the church as we know it was on the way out. They had their backs to the wall. It looked like the darkest day in the history of the church in North America. But something changed. There was a shift. A movement of prayer and fasting broke out and soon after this movement of prayer and fasting one of the greatest revivals the world has seen swept through the world. It's like certain leaders of the church in that day realised that if they didn't do something radical to change future outcomes then the church was gone.

Fasting is an invitation from God to change future outcomes on planet earth. It is an opportunity to work with God in a shift. We see this in the New Testament within the Acts 13 encounter but it is also clearly seen throughout the pages of the Old Testament. There is situation after situation in the Old Testament where people changed history as they prayed and fasted. Up to now I have reasoned that Old and New Testament fasting is fundamentally different because of the way Jesus changes it, but in this function of fasting the new mirrors the old and we see a sense of continuum.

It is considered by some that the issue of fasting for change in the events of history is marginal in the New Testament. It is thought to be marginal based on the lack of volume of texts that discuss it.[61] Volume of texts however can be misleading in determining the value of a particular text. It is true that there are not many texts about fasting after the gospels, and even less when we consider changing history through fasting. However, the texts that are present on fasting often seem to have important salvation historical events attached to them.

One such occasion is recorded in Acts 13: 1-3. The text reads;

> *¹ Now in the church at Antioch there were prophets and teachers: Barnabas, Simeon called Niger, Lucius of Cyrene, Manaen (who had been brought up with Herod the tetrarch) and Saul. ² While they were worshiping the Lord and fasting, the Holy Spirit said, "Set apart for me Barnabas and Saul for the work to which I have called them." ³ So after they had fasted and prayed, they placed their hands on them and sent them off.* [62]

The prophets and teachers of the church of Antioch were worshipping the Lord and fasting. It was in this context that The Holy Spirit spoke to them and commissioned Saul and Barnabas for their missionary trip. The text may not be very long but the impact of this fast can be felt today.

> *Fasting in Acts 13 changed the course of history. It is almost impossible to overstate the historical importance of that moment in the history of the world. Before this word from the Holy Spirit, there seems to be no organised mission beyond the eastern*

---

61 I. H. Marshall, *Jesus-Example and Teacher of Prayer in the Synoptic Gospels* in R. N. Longnecker, (ed.) *Into God's Presence: Prayer in the New Testament* (Grand Rapids, Mich.: William B. Eerdmans, 2001) 125.
62 THE HOLY BIBLE, NEW INTERNATIONAL VERSION®, NIV® Copyright © 1973, 1978, 1984, 2011 by Biblica, Inc.™

> *seacoast of the Mediterranean. Before this, Paul had made no missionary journeys westward to Asia Minor, Greece, Rome or Spain. Before this Paul had not written any of his letters, which were all a result of his missionary travels, which began here. This moment of prayer and fasting resulted in a missions movement that would catapult Christianity from obscurity into being the dominant religion of the Roman Empire within two and a half centuries.*[63]

This fasting at important times seems to be a pattern that they continue as they travel and plant churches throughout Asia Minor.[64] With every church plant that was established throughout Acts they would appoint elders through the process of prayer and fasting according to Acts 14:23. It reads;

> *23 Paul and Barnabas appointed elders[a] for them in each church and, with prayer and fasting, committed them to the Lord, in whom they had put their trust.*[65]

This mirrors the encounter in Acts 13. In view here is not some ritual but a dynamic fasting in which the Holy Spirit's leading and guidance was central.[66] It was very different to the fasting that the Jews would undertake. Regular fasting for Israel initially occurred only on one day a year, the Day of Atonement.[67] This fasting on the Day of Atonement,

---

63 Piper, *A Hunger for God: Desiring God through Fasting and Prayer* 107.
64 W. Grudem, *Systematic Theology* (Bath, England: IVP, 1994) 390.
65 THE HOLY BIBLE, NEW INTERNATIONAL VERSION®, NIV® Copyright © 1973, 1978, 1984, 2011 by Biblica, Inc.™
66 Lachman, and Smith, (Eds) *Worship in the Presence of God* 267.
67 Daniel J. Harrington, *To Fast or not to Fast* America, 2/20/2006, Vol. 194 Issue 6, p30.

or as it was called Yom Kippur, had an atoning function[68] for their sins.[69] That was an annual fast for one day whereas this is fasting to gain the guidance of the Holy Spirit. It wasn't like the elders of the church couldn't shake off the tradition of fasting. What we see here is Spirit led fasting that was driving forward the process of the church growing and changing the course of history. It was dynamic, Spirit led and impacting the world so it would never be the same again.

## Joel 2

This theme of fasting being part of the hinge of history is fairly common in the Old Testament story. The most telling story being that of Joel 2. Joel 2 presents a radically different scenario concerning fasting and the post-exilic period compared to other places in the Old Testament. Where Zechariah had a focus on the fact that one day, fasting as mourning would be finished, and rejoicing would be the mark of the people of God and Isaiah had a focus that the fast be from the heart and not mere ritual. Joel presents an urgent call for the whole community to fast in the light of a national disaster.

The fasting that is called for in Joel 2 functions as sign of mourning and repentance.[70] It is a trumpet call for the people of God to return to Him and partner in turning history around. It reads;

---

68 Whether the supposed atoning function exists in the act itself of fasting or is part of the overall process will be discussed in the corresponding section on Leviticus 16
69 D. S. Ben Ezra, *Whose Fast is it?* in A. H. Becker,. and A. Y. Reed, (Eds) *The ways that never parted: Jews and Christians in late antiquity and the early Middle Ages* (Minneapolis, Minn.: Fortress Press, 2007) 277.
70 R. B. Chisholm, *Interpreting the Minor Prophets* (Grand Rapids, Mich. : Zondervan Publishing House, 1990) 59-60.

*Blow the trumpet in Zion,*
   *declare a holy fast,*
   *call a sacred assembly.*
*16 Gather the people,*
   *consecrate the assembly;*
*bring together the elders,*
   *gather the children,*
   *those nursing at the breast.*
*Let the bridegroom leave his room*
   *and the bride her chamber.*
*17 Let the priests, who minister before the LORD,*
   *weep between the portico and the altar.*
*Let them say, "Spare your people, LORD.*
   *Do not make your inheritance an object of scorn,*
   *a byword among the nations.*
*Why should they say among the peoples,*
   *'Where is their God?'"* [71]

Within verses 15 to 17 seven imperatives are issued in staccato fashion with specific directions about what is expected from the people of God. The lawful things are to be set aside for the purpose of fasting.[72] The message from Joel is clear that God's people are apostate and as a result they are suffering under the hand of God. The whole of the community are suffering and are called to lament and mourn.[73]

---

71 THE HOLY BIBLE, NEW INTERNATIONAL VERSION®, NIV® Copyright © 1973, 1978, 1984, 2011 by Biblica, Inc.™

72 O. P. Robertson, *Prophet of the coming day of the Lord : the message of Joel*. (Durham, NC: Evangelical Press, 1995) 55-56.

73 E. Achtemeier, *Minor prophets I : N.I.B.C.* (Peabody, Mass. : Hendrickson Publishers, 1996) 125.

In the same way that the whole of the community is suffering so the whole community is being called to repent and fast. 'So important is the meeting that all the shareholders in the covenant ...must be present...so serious is the crisis that a normal privilege is temporarily withdrawn'.[74] So vital was this call that it was heralded with the sound of the trumpet which was usually reserved for royal inaugurations, raising the army or a cultic procession.[75] As well as the call for all to come and fast in verse 17, 'the call to the priests is distinctive in this section in that it singles them out for a special task, they are to intercede for the nation'.[76] We are presented with a picture saying that it was not business as usual. Everybody was to stop what they were doing and come. Even the mother who was breastfeeding. As well as the couple who had just said their wedding vows and were on their way to consummate the marriage. It is a picture of urgency. There are no excuses and nobody is exempt.

The priests are especially in Joel's view. So often the temperature of the people of God is set by those who have been commissioned to spiritually care for them. We are left with little question after reading Joel that something is amiss with the priests. But God is calling them to lead again and weep as an act of intercession before God.

Along with this Joel 2 encounter one of the common features of the Old Testament narrative is that fasting functions as a way of asking God for assistance with national disasters. It is a critical factor in moments of history turning around.

---

74 L. C. Allen, *The books of Joel, Obadiah, Jonah and Micah NICOT* (London : Hodder & Stoughton, 1976) 82-3.
75 T. E. McComiskey, *The Minor Prophets : an exegetical and expository commentary. Volume 1 : Hosea, Joel and Amos* (Grand Rapids, Mich.: Baker Book House, 1992) 283.
76 D. A. Garrett, *Hosea, Joel. New American commentary* (U.S.A: Broadman & Holman, 1997) 349.

## Esther

The book of Esther shows us another point in the history of the Jews when their very existence is under threat. There is a plot to destroy the Jews and Esther has been placed into a position of influence. So faced with the destruction of the Jews and so much weight on her shoulders she intuitively calls a fast. Esther 4:15-16 says

> *[15] Then Esther sent this reply to Mordecai: [16] "Go, gather together all the Jews who are in Susa, and fast for me. Do not eat or drink for three days, night or day. I and my attendants will fast as you do. When this is done, I will go to the king, even though it is against the law. And if I perish, I perish."*[77]

The fast in this instance functions to prepare Esther for her history changing moment with the king. It not only prepares Esther but also is a vital point in the narrative in turning the whole story in the favour of the Jews. It is really important here again to see that the fast is not a ritual but a desperate response. What is telling is that nobody tells her to fast. God does not speak, Mordecai does not tell her. She just knows that God responds to heartfelt fasting. So a three day fast turns the history of the world around.

## Jonah

The context for Jonah 3 is quite different to that of Esther but we still see a situation in which history is turned around by people fasting. Jonah has been told to go to Nineveh and up to this point had resisted. However he does go and calls out that the city is about to be destroyed.

> *Jonah began by going a day's journey into the city, proclaiming,*

---

[77] THE HOLY BIBLE, NEW INTERNATIONAL VERSION®, NIV® Copyright © 1973, 1978, 1984, 2011 by Biblica, Inc.™

> *"Forty more days and Nineveh will be overthrown."* ⁵ *The Ninevites believed God. A fast was proclaimed, and all of them, from the greatest to the least, put on sackcloth.*
>
> ⁶ *When Jonah's warning reached the king of Nineveh, he rose from his throne, took off his royal robes, covered himself with sackcloth and sat down in the dust.* ⁷ *This is the proclamation he issued in Nineveh:*
>
> *"By the decree of the king and his nobles:*
>
> *Do not let people or animals, herds or flocks, taste anything; do not let them eat or drink.* ⁸ *But let people and animals be covered with sackcloth. Let everyone call urgently on God. Let them give up their evil ways and their violence.* ⁹ *Who knows? God may yet relent and with compassion turn from his fierce anger so that we will not perish."* [78]

Again we see a situation in which a people intuitively know to fast in order to turn the moment around and these people were not even God's own people. Jonah doesn't even declare a fast. The first moment a fast is mentioned is when the text says that the Ninevites believed God and declared a fast. We know that God hears them and turns from the judgement that he had declared. History had been turned in an incredible set of circumstances.

So Joel, Esther and Jonah all contain instances where the response of the people is to fast.[79] In some of these cases the people intuitively know what to do and in some of the cases they are told how to repent. In each

---

[78] THE HOLY BIBLE, NEW INTERNATIONAL VERSION®, NIV® Copyright © 1973, 1978, 1984, 2011 by Biblica, Inc.™

[79] Smith-Christopher, *Fasting* in Freedman & Myers (Ed) *Eerdmans dictionary of the Bible* 456.

of the cases assistance is needed, either because of the people's sin or the sin of other nations.

But back in Joel 2 we are given an important insight into the process of repentance and intercession for a nation in post-exilic times. Some might say that all these other cases of fasting in this era concerning the destruction of nations could be explained as descriptive. That is, the writer of the text is not saying fasting is good or bad or otherwise just that the people did it. These people might say it was common to all cultures to fast and it was really the repentance that is important.

Joel 2 becomes even more important in this context because it seems to be prescriptive. That is the only place in the narrative where we get an insight into God's perspective of fasting. He wants it to happen. 'The only other fast, which is ordained by God, besides the Day of Atonement fast, is recorded by Joel.'[80] Is it possible that Joel therefore functions as a commentary or editorial on all the other recorded acts of fasting in the post-exilic era? Whereas all the other recorded fasts in this era have some sort of chronological markers, Joel does not. There is no date in the superscription and a noticeable absence of important temporal references within the book. The plague of locusts does not help us date the book as these types of events were commonplace.[81]

> *Ultimately, however it should be remembered that the importance of dating the book for the purpose of interpretation is minimal. Unlike the nature of other prophecies in which knowledge of time and history is significantly related to its understanding, the message of Joel is timeless. It forms a doctrine that could be repeated and applied in any age*[82]

---

80 Chatham, *Fasting: A Biblical Historical Study* 31.

81 I. A. Busenitz, *Joel and Obadiah* (Great Britain: CFP, 2003) 11-12.

82 Busenitz, *Joel and Obadiah* 34.

So it is conceivable that in some way Joel functions to bring understanding and perspective to the many instances of fasting we witness in the Old Testament narrative. Joel has timeless themes and is one of the only times that fasting is viewed as an imperative.

History shifts when we respond to the invitation of God to fast over our present circumstances. Esther knew it and proved God powerful and faithful to deliver her nation. Jonah saw it first hand as the mediator between a city that was destined to be wiped out and God. Joel gave us a timeless answer for when history seems out of control. The answer that is always current. Call the elders and the people and fast and cry out to God for a shift. The question now beckons, what are you going to do about your nation, city, church or family? The options seem to be limited. Either declare that the process of sin is in fact the will of God, throw our hands up in despair or drop everything and respond to the holy invitation of heaven to be the hinge of history. It is not too big for God. Whatever challenge you face he is just waiting to partner with you. But it might mean you need to drop something. You might need to drop your pride. You might need to drop your self assurance. You might need to drop your theological worldview that says God doesn't do this sort of thing. Whatever it is, drop it and answer the call of heaven. Many before us, such as Jonathan Edwards, heard the invitation of heaven and ended up causing seismic shifts in history. He and past warriors have gone now but you are here. You can stand in the gap between where the planet is today and where God wants to take it. This is the period of history you are responsible for. You are the custodian for the world we will pass on to our children and their children. So, what are you going to do about that?

We see a church in Acts 13 that takes that invitation and responsibly very seriously. We see a church that understands the power that is released when we pray and fast. We see a church that is not afraid to respond to the invitation of heaven. As a result the world is turned on its head. It is time for another revolution. It is time for another reformation. This Acts 13 fast started a chain of events that saw the gospel taken everywhere in the next 300 years. It transformed people, cities and whole cultures. It transformed families. It transformed cities. It transformed government. From the smallest to the largest. All spheres. It is time again to see such a push. It is time to see revolution released. It is time to take the DNA of the Acts 13 church and inject it back into the sleeping giant that is the church of the 21$^{st}$ century. Now is our time. RSVP to the invitation of heaven!

# 5.

# INVITATION TO DO JUSTICE

Have you every done something so many times that you stop asking questions about why you are doing it. It can happen in any sphere of life. The activity that you once had to take time over because it took every ounce of your concentration has become so routine that you can do it without thinking. A bit like driving into your driveway and not remembering the last five minutes because you were deep in thought and then thinking "How did it get here?". Last thing you remember you were several blocks away and then you stopped concentrating on the task at hand. It's like you have switched onto autopilot. You are still doing the task required but any thought process and passion about it have long gone.

It is not just the physical sphere of life that we can switch on the autopilot. It can happen in the area of the spiritual as well. It can even happen in the area of fasting. That might be a bit hard for you to swallow because fasting can be so physically demanding. However, it is true that any spiritual discipline can become about the form and not the heart, and therefore meaningless. This process is a sure-fire way for any activity to become about other reasons than the original reasons.

Isaiah 58 presents us with a people who have gone into autopilot when it comes to spiritual issues. It is a picture of people who have lost the true meaning of fasting and accepted a thinly veneered religious practice that was all about trying to look good in the eyes of man. It is a grave picture of how ritual can lose meaning and religious acts can be preformed without heart as though one is just going through the motions.[83]

Isaiah 58 opens with God voicing his displeasure at the way that something is playing out amongst his people. He tells the prophet to let them know about his displeasure. Verse three is the voice of the Israelites and their complaint before the Lord

> **3a** '*Why have we fasted, and you see it not? Why have we humbled ourselves, and you take no knowledge of it?*'

It appears that the people of God had been fasting but that God wasn't very moved by it. It is totally possible that we engage in something but God is not moved by it. Personally I don't want to spend a moment engaging in something that misses the heart of God. That is what makes this interaction so fascinating. God is not moved by their fasting. They had been fasting. So on a purely action level they were keeping the letter of the law. But their hearts are far from it. God answered them, but not in the way they were expecting.

> **3b** *Behold, in the day of your fast you seek your own pleasure, and oppress all your workers.*
> **4***Behold, you fast only to quarrel and to fight and to hit with a wicked fist. Fasting like yours this day will not make your voice to be heard on high.*

---

[83] Rothenberg, *Fast* in C. Brown (Ed) *The new international dictionary of New Testament Theology*.

'God was tired with the Israelites' pretence of worship'.[84] God answers their question with a critique of how their fasting was not true. They are disappointed that God is not listening to them and answering them in their customary fasting days. They are unaware that their behaviour is displeasing to God.[85] God had not answered them and was displeased with them that they ignored the true intention of the fast days and went about their secular activities.[86] Isaiah speaks to a religion that is superficial and not of the heart.[87] The people of God misunderstood what was acceptable to God. They had forgotten about mercy to the poor and needy. Self sacrifice that has a real and tangible effect for others is better than self sacrifice that benefits nobody.[88]

> **5** *Is such the fast that I choose, a day for a person to humble himself? Is it to bow down his head like a reed, and to spread sackcloth and ashes under him? Will you call this a fast, and a day acceptable to the LORD?* **6** *"Is not this the fast that I choose: to loose the bonds of wickedness, to undo the straps of the yoke to let the oppressed go free, and to break every yoke?* **7** *Is it not to share your bread with the hungry and bring the homeless poor into your house; when you see the naked, to cover him, and not to hide yourself from your own flesh?*

God is not pleased with their fasting. However, it is important to note that it was not the fasting per se that God was unhappy about so much

---

84 Chatham, *Fasting: A Biblical Historical Study* 25.
85 Whybray, *Isaiah 40-66 NCBC* 211-212.
86 Whybray, *Isaiah 40-66 NCBC* 211-212.
87 J. N. Oswalt, The *Book of Isaiah: Chapters 40-66* (Grand Rapids, USA: Eerdmans Pub. Co., 1998) 494-495.
88 Whybray, *Isaiah 40-66 NCBC* 221.

as the heart behind it. Within the biblical text there is no condemnation of fasting as such, but rather of using it as a substitute for looking after the poor.[89] 'Regardless of Isaiah's feelings about the abuse of fasting, it is obvious that he recognised it as a legitimate form of worship, and that he found no fault with it being carried out on specially called occasions.'[90] The question being asked in this context is about effectual fasting.

Israel wanted to know why fasting was not working and God tells them. If it were to function as true worship and manifest as care for the poor then it would please God.[91] In this way their fasting would not have just been about personal piety but rather it would have been a prophetic witness of the whole community as to the nature of God in providing for the poor and needy.[92] In this way fasting takes on a function of social justice because true fasting was about taking the meal you were going to eat and giving to the hungry.[93] This is no small point. The link between the spiritual action of fasting and the social justice function of fasting. The two were to go hand in hand, yet somehow had become divorced from each other and as such God wasn't pleased.

This theme of linking the spiritual act of fasting to the social justice outcome of feeding the poor and needy is not confined to the Old Testament. I wonder when Jesus starts teaching on the Sermon on the Mount, whether Isaiah 58 comes to remembrance very quickly for the hearers. In Matthew chapter six we see Jesus link together three topics that at first glance don't seem very connected. They were: giving to the poor and needy, prayer and fasting. So how do we know they are

---

89 Whybray, *Isaiah 40-66 NCBC* 221.

90 Merrill,. *Fasting* in W. A. Elwell, *Evangelical dictionary of theology* 246.

91 C. Westermann, *Isaiah 40-66* (Philadelphia, Pa.: Westminster Press, 1987) 333.

92 E. Duffy. *To Fast Again* First Things, no 151 March 2005, p 4-6

93 T. Ryan, *Fasting: A Fresh Look*. America, 3/6/2006, Vol. 194 Issue 8, p8-12,

connected? After all, the modern text has a big heading separating these topics to highlight a new thought. There seems to be a thematic and a syntax connection. The primary thematic connection point for Jesus' listeners was that all three of these where being used by the Pharisees to get the approval of man. These were all spiritual activities that were expected, but just like in Isaiah 58 the passion for God has gone out of them. They have becomes a means for the Pharisees to serve their own interests. The syntax connection is that verse one is a warning and then the three different areas are connected by "and", meaning that they are all linked to the big idea of making it about God and not man.

So we see a connection between fasting and feeding the poor and needy. It is spelt out by Isaiah and reinforced by Jesus. Jesus doesn't seem to add any new twist or reinterpretation, which would indicate that the idea of forgoing a meal and giving to somebody else is still in force. In this way fasting becomes an act of social justice. It becomes a tangible act of the concern that God has for the poor and needy. It becomes an invitation for us, in the modern age, to continue the practice of caring for those less well off through our fasting. It also becomes an invitation for those of us who are well fed to experience for the moment what it is like not to have food in our bellies. In this way it becomes a powerful catalyst for change. It is one thing to hear about taking care of the poor. It is another thing all together to go without food for a meal or two and then remember those for whom this is normal. In this way it serves to stir the wealthy out of our culture of comfort and intercede in a real way for the poor masses of the world. Who knows what movements of social justice can be stirred by identification like this?

We live in the day of the fridge so if you miss a meal you can just store it in the fridge or freezer and have it at a later time. In this way its like we aren't really missing out at all. But this wasn't the case for those in Jesus' day. There was very little chance to store the food. So you became very aware when you were missing meals that the food should go to somebody else. This was and is the plan of God to provide for the poor. That you and I would go without for a time so those with little can enjoy and be nourished. It is a holy invitation on a whole different level to engage with the heart of God in social action. So next time you plan to fast why don't you do something about the food you would have eaten and in so doing change the world a little bit at a time.

# 6.

# INVITATION TO DIE TO SELF

If you want your book to be a bestseller these days you have to have a catchy title that is really "up". It appeals to people to read something like "Your best life now" or something like that. If you want to make sure your book doesn't sell, then maybe a title like "Die to self" would be perfect. There is something about the concept that seems really uncomfortable and just plain painful. It tends to bring up images of God just being really mean to us. The reality is however that it is essential that each one of us lay our life down in order that we would fully experience the life of God flowing through us. That is the process of dying to self and living fully for God. It is the process of consecration. God issues an invitation to us to come die to self and live fully for him, and I have found that the most intense moments in my life when this is happening are in the times of fasting. It is like God just starts stripping away everything and goes to work on making us more like him.

This idea of dying to self is really all about dying to the sin desire that lives in us. It isn't about standing in front of a bus and wishing you were dead so much as taking every effort to make sure the sin nature is dead. This link between fasting, consecration and dealing with the sin in our lives is not a concept that is new in the New Testament, but finds it roots in the Old Testament.

It is in the book of Leviticus that we see the root of this link between the three concepts. We see in Leviticus that a requirement is made that fasting is carried out in a specific and ongoing way.[94] There were many cases of fasting in the Old Testament, but the function and full meaning of those fasts is something that mostly needs to be determined from the context.[95] Some of these fasts appear to be descriptive of an event rather that prescriptive as to common practice. The Day of Atonement changes all this as it is the first occurrence of an explicit command to fast.[96] Leviticus 16:29-31 says

> *And it shall be a statute to you forever that in the seventh month, on the tenth day of the month, you shall afflict yourselves\* and shall do no work, either the native or the stranger who sojourns among you. For on this day shall atonement be made for you to cleanse you? You shall be clean before the LORD from all your sins. It is a Sabbath of solemn rest to you, and you shall afflict yourselves\*; it is a statute forever.*
> *\*Or shall fast (ESV)*

This was the one day of the year in which the Israelites were not to eat and not to work. The phrase 'afflict yourself[97]' meant to fast within

---

94 Harrington, *To Fast or not to Fast* America, 2/20/2006, Vol. 194 Issue 6, p30.
95 Smith-Christopher, *Fasting* in Freedman, & Myers, (Ed) *Eerdmans dictionary of the Bible* 456.
96 Chatham, *Fasting: A Biblical Historical Study* 4-6.
97 The main word translated as 'fast' in the Old Testament is the Hebrew word *Tsum* and means 'to afflict oneself'. Muddiman says that 'to afflict oneself' was a periphrastic construction that meant 'fast' within the Priestly code. Merrill concurs by commenting on the verb. 'is the only one used to describe fasting as a religious experience. It conveys the explicit meaning "to abstain from food" and thus occurs regularly as a technical religious term'. Rothenberg and Grun were not as definitive as Muddiman and Merrill.

the priestly context. It was a day of Sabbath rest in which burnt offerings were made and sins were confessed for the previous year. This fasting didn't atone for the sins but it was part of the atoning process.[98] That is, the fasting prepared the people for the atonement by causing them to mourn over their sin and consecrate themselves for the ritual. In was in the process of fasting that they became acutely aware of the weight of sin. It is highly possible that we can go day to day and not give sin a thought but something about the process of fasting causes a renewed awareness.

Much later in Israel's history, during the period between the Testaments, in the mind of some Jews, fasting had moved from the function of preparing for the Day of Atonement to actually atoning for sin. The Psalms of Solomon 3: 6-8 says that fasting will atone for the sin of ignorance.[99] In the mind of some Jews scribes, fasting had the function of atoning for their sins. It only seems like a small shift but the implications are huge. It moves fasting from being a preparatory element to being the whole deal. This is something that can easily happen with many helpful disciplines. They can go from being preparatory to being the main deal. It is crucial that we never allow fasting to become a good

---

They agreed with the verb meaning fasting but without the reference to priestly context. Smith-Christopher says the verb is often taken to include fasting. Blunt says it usually means to fast. There is consensus that the verb means 'fast', however some of the scholars infer that in other contexts it does not mean fast. However, while they say there are exceptions they fail to site them. So it appears that outside the priestly context 'to afflict oneself' could have a wide range of meaning while also functioning as a priestly idiom for a religious fast. Within the Old Testament 'fast' was used in a range of settings from purification to oppression from great cares to how to respond to national crisis.

98 Chatham, *Fasting: A Biblical Historical Study* 2-3.
99 D. E. Garland, *Mark in Zondervan Illustrated Bible backgrounds commentary* (Grand Rapids, Mich.: Zondervan, 2002) 222.

work for which we gain "brownie points" from God. Here it its original context it was designed to soften the heart and lead to greater devotion.

You may have attempted to look up the last reference I quoted in your bible. You might have checked Psalm 3 and not found it. You might have then checked Song of Solomon 3 and still not found it. Maybe you were thinking that it is a misprint. You probably won't find it as the Psalm of Solomon is part of the Pseudepigraphical Jewish Literature. As such it is not considered part of the bible and is therefore without the weight of authority that the bible carries. 'Psalms (of Solomon) are the product of an unknown Jewish sect, living in Jerusalem in the first century BCE who oppose the temple priesthood and consider it illegitimate'.[100] This text for a few reasons should not inform our discussion of the function of fasting. Firstly, it was written over a thousand years later that the Leviticus text with a different context and setting and therefore cannot seen to be for interpreting the Day of Atonement text. Secondly it comes within a body of writing that is rejected by most scholars as to being part of the authoritative word of God. Lastly it was written by a group that was anti-temple and therefore is biased against orthodox understanding as presented in Leviticus. We can safely say then that the invitation to fast is not about atoning for sin but rather *cutting our heart over sin* and encouraging consecration.

This atonement ceremony of Yom Kippur or the Day of Atonement still continues for some Jews today. At the end of the street I lived in was an Orthodox Synagogue. We knew that Yom Kippur was approaching because the letterbox started to fill up with ads about the High Holidays as well as Christian tracts discussing how to truly be atoned for. The

---

[100] L. L. Grabbe, *I Cried to the Lord: A Study of the Psalms of Solomon's Historical Background and Social Setting.* Journal for the Study of the Old Testament, June 2005, Vol. 29 Issue 5, p177.

New Testament Christian has a different view of Yom Kippur as there is a radical new understanding for the Day of Atonement for Christians. Christians understand that the final atoning work for the sin of man has been completed on the cross and there is now no need to continue the practice of the Day of Atonement.

The patristic church seemed to understand this new atonement as well so they initiated a new fast, the Ember Day fasts, to compete with Yom Kippur.[101] So while the Jews were celebrating Yom Kippur in the years after Jesus' ministry on earth, the early church would fast at the same time but with a very different focus. The Roman lectionary of the Ember Days had the 'final epistolary reading of the Saturday vigil Hebrews 9:2-12 depicting Jesus Christ[102] performing the high priest's ritual from the Day of Atonement'.[103] The lectionary was constructed in such a way that there was a typological connection between Leviticus 16 and Hebrews 9. The connection was deliberate and incredibly powerful. While the Jews were performing the high priestly duties in the synagogue the church was celebrating that fulfilment just across the street. This Hebrews reading was presented as the apex of the reading cycle 'communicating to the hearer that Christ himself undertakes the atoning work of the true Yom Kippur'.[104] As a result the Ember Day fast was not about reproducing the atoning function of Christ but remembering it and celebrating it. In the same way that fasting in

---

101 Ben Ezra, *Whose Fast is it?* in Becker,. and Reed, (Eds) *The ways that never parted: Jews and Christians in late antiquity and the early Middle Ages* 279.
102 V. Buksbazen, *The Gospel and the Feasts of Israel.* (Collingswood, N.J: Spearhead Press, 1972) 33.
103 Ben Ezra, *Whose Fast is it?* in Becker & Reed, (Eds) *The ways that never parted: Jews and Christians in late antiquity and the early Middle Ages* 277.
104 Ben Ezra, *Whose Fast is it?* in Becker & Reed, (Eds) *The ways that never parted: Jews and Christians in late antiquity and the early Middle Ages* 277.

Leviticus functioned to mourn for sin and prepare the person for the ritual, so the Ember Day fast was about remembrance and response to what Christ had done and making that atonement a reality but acting out the consecration and desire to die to that sin.

This understanding of the atonement, while being clear in the liturgy and practice of the church was still being challenged by sections of the patristic church. Romanos the Melodist proposed the idea that fasting within Lent had an atoning function. He saw fasting as possibly atoning for the original sin that some believed was caused by gluttony in Paradise.[105] Ambrose also agreed with this reasoning that fasting atoned for original sin.[106] However, the context for their writings is interesting and sheds some light on what they might have been reacting to in their writings and thoughts.

Romanos and Ambrose were writing in a time of great moral laxity amongst the Catholic Church. It was also a period of history in which the ascetic lifestyle was highly valued by some. The worldview behind the ascetic lifestyle was that food was bad or evil and should be avoided as much as possible and fasting could do this. It is a view of food that is not supported by the Bible as God encouraged Adam to eat from all the trees but one. We know that God has given us food to grow the human body and sustain us. Paul encourages us not to allow it to master us with the idea being it is a good gift of God but our appetite must be managed.

Rather this ascetic view has its basis in Plato's thinking which separates the material from the spiritual; the material being evil and

---

[105] Allen, Canning, & Cross, (Eds) *Prayer and Spirituality in the Early Church. Volume 1* (Everton Park, Qld: Centre for Early Christian Studies, Australian Catholic University, 1998) 216.

[106] Allen, Canning, & Cross, (Eds) *Prayer and Spirituality in the Early Church. Volume 1* (Everton Park, Qld: Centre for Early Christian Studies, Australian Catholic University, 1998) 214.

the spiritual being good. The biblical reality is that food is good and has been created for our pleasure and sustenance but with any good gift of God we are reminded to not let it rule over us and control us.[107] These writers were reading gluttony into the Genesis text so they could write polemically against the excesses of their day. There is no support biblically that fasting has an atoning function within the church age. They were also reading gluttony into the first temptation of Jesus texts in the gospel narrative. The reality is that Jesus was not being tempted to gluttony because 'what kind of high living is there in bread'[108].

This idea of fasting as an invitation to die to sin and consecrate oneself finds it way into the New Testament text as well. When we see the prophets and teachers of the Antiochan church fasting in Acts 13: 1-3 we see a link between fasting and worship. The text says that they were worshipping the Lord and fasting. Without a big discussion about whether worship is an act or a lifestyle, we still see a link. It is interesting that Paul, who is bodily present at this moment of fasting and history, is the same one who pens in Romans about the essence of worship. He says in Romans 12: 1 to present your bodies as a living sacrifice to God, which is your spiritual worship. Interesting is that he doesn't say to present yourself. That would imply the whole self like body, soul and mine. In view here is the physical body not doing what it would naturally want to do, but rather as an act of worship to God. Within that we could understand to abstain from sinful practice but also to abstain from the good as well for a time to cause the body to be a living sacrifice of worship.

When we fast we learn to say No. It is not a really popular concept

---

107 1 Corinthians 6: 12-20
108 J. Calvin, *A harmony of the Gospels Matthew, Mark and Luke. Volume 1 /* (Grand Rapids, Mich.: William B. Eerdmans, 1980) 137.

today. We seem to be a society that gives into every little whim. If we see something, we want it and not only that we have become a society in which we must have it right now. The western world seems more overvieght than at any other time of history. We live in a day in which the delay of gratification seems to be obsolete. But this ability to delay gratification is an essential part of success. It is widely recognised in business now that those who can say 'no' or 'later' will generally be more successful that those who cannot.

The heart of fasting is saying no to something that is perfectly OK for a time in order to do business with God. It is essential that we can say no to sin and fasting helps develop this ability to control our bodies. It develops the ability to instead of having the stomach and our appetites master us that we master them. This is at the heart of what Paul says in Romans 12: 1. True worship is the ability to say no to the natural desires of the body when they scream at us to indulge in a wrong context or in an excessive manor. In this way fasting and worship and putting to dead the works of the flesh are all linked.

Jesus even issued a blessing for this type of fasting. He said in the beatitudes that *Blessed are those who hunger and thirst for righteousness, for they will be filled.* Interesting here that Jesus is not just talking about those who are forced to go hungry as the mood is active rather than passive. It is about those who are actively going without the good in order to get the better. The reason they are going without food and drink is in order that the righteousness of God might become a greater reality in them. The better for them, is that they are filled. They will be filled with righteousness and that will spill out in being blessed. Blessed in its most simplest form means to be made happy. Jesus is saying that those who fast in order that they might do business with God concerning the sin in their lives will experience power to see the sin broken and then they will be filled with all happiness as a result. God's righteousness becoming a greater reality even in the hidden parts of our lives is certainly something to be filled with joy and happiness about.

God is always issuing the Holy invitation to say No. It is not as cool as other aspects of the invitation. It is not as funky as changing history or greater empowerment but never the less it is His invitation and it will produce a world of benefits as we learn to lay our body down on the alter of worship. Go ahead and respond. Ask him to help you to RSVP to this most crucial aspect of his invitation. You will be thankful every time you avoid pitfalls because your body is trained in righteousness and holy living.

# 7.

# INVITATION TO LISTEN

If you are anything like me there are times in your life when it is really difficult to discern what God is saying and doing. There comes whose moments in life where you really need the wisdom of God. There comes lots of moments. I'm not talking about things that God has clearly said in the Bible. We can thank him that he has made himself really clear on some issues. I'm talking about everyday questions, issues and problems that you really want to hear what God says. There can be really painful moments when we admit to ourselves that our ears are dull and so often cannot hear what God is saying.

Maybe you are asking God about which country he wants you to serve in or which university to attend. It might be what ministry to get involved in or how much to spend on a certain item. You might be asking what to do about a wayward child or how to handle some stinging criticism. Every day in a many different contexts you get an opportunity to ask God about the matters that concern you. If you are like me many times we don't hear an answer.

So in the absence of an answer we tend to form a theology. We say things like; God doesn't speak outside the Bible these days or you aren't asking specifically enough or God is being silent to test you and grow you. All of these answers sound spiritual enough except they directly go against what the scriptures say. James in Chapter 1 makes it really clear about the nature of God when it comes to speaking to his children.

> *If any of you lacks wisdom, you should ask God, who gives generously to all without finding fault, and it will be given to you. [6] But when you ask, you must believe and not doubt, because the one who doubts is like a wave of the sea, blown and tossed by the wind. [7] That person should not expect to receive anything from the Lord. [8] Such a person is double-minded and unstable in all they do.*[109]

It is really clear from this passage about the nature of God. He loves to speak to his children even when he could find fault and rebuke us. Instead he speaks generously. The idea of God speaking generously paints an awesome picture of God just leaning forward waiting for us to say *Help, what do I do here?* And then he answers with a heart full of love. The passage also shows us how we should ask. The main condition is to not doubt that God is a speaking God and that his heart is to speak to you on any subject at any time in any context. So we just need to affirm that he loves to speak and not move from that position. God is a speaking God and any other theology is just a poor substitute derived from experiences of not hearing God.

So James is clear, God speaks today. Paul backs this up in his dealing with the Corinthian church by asking the prophets to keep it to just 2 or 3 each service. The inference being that you could go on for days if you didn't limit it. So why don't we hear him more often? I wonder if it is that our ears are so dull and our spiritual senses are numbed by the lifestyle

---

[109] THE HOLY BIBLE, NEW INTERNATIONAL VERSION®, NIV® Copyright © 1973, 1978, 1984, 2011 by Biblica, Inc.™

that we live. God is always speaking but are we always tuned in. I was having trouble hearing God a while back so I tried an exercise in my car. I have about a 45 minutes commute each way to my office, so I decided to stop listening to the radio on the commute. In fact I stopped listening to everything. No radio, no podcast, no worship music. Nothing. It's like my ears were taking a fast. I didn't do it for just a day or two but ended up doing it for about four months. At times I would find myself praying but other times I just sat in silence.

It was such a wonderful experience in stopping and allowing my ears to become sharp again. We often ask God to speak but then don't give a moment to hear. I'm not saying that we must stop and be perfectly still every time we wish an answer from God. When I did my 4 month ear fast, I had a full time job, Pastored a church plant, had four kids and wife and was about to start a company. Life is full but I find God speaking to me all the time. What I'm talking about is if you are finding it hard to hear then its time to stop.

Sometimes it is not only helpful to stop in order to hear God but it is also helpful to stop eating in order to hear God. As I reflect on the account in Acts 13 and the setting aside of Paul and Barnabas I am amazed how fasting and hearing what the Holy Spirit is saying goes hand in hand. The prophets and teachers were fasting and worshipping and in that context then Holy Spirit speaks to them a word that changes the history of the world. I wonder if this is the first time that something like this has happened to them but we find out a chapter later that has become standard practice for the leaders of the church to fast and hear God about who should be placed into leadership. Acts 14: 23 says *Paul and Barnabas appointed elders for them in each church and, with prayer and fasting, committed them to the Lord, in whom they had put their trust.*[110] In other words they were so impacted by their Acts 13 encounter with the clarity of the voice of the Holy Spirit that they started doing this in each of the churches they started. So they would take some time to pray and fast and then God would speak to them. Without fail. But the key for Paul and Barnabas here is that they had to stop in order to hear. So eating, which fuels activity, would cease for a time and they would just tune the ears and spiritual senses into the God who speaks.

I have found that a sharpness comes in my spirit when I fast like no other time I know. It's like the distraction of food is put aside and I can really focus in on God. The difference between a time of fasting and a few days later is very noticeable. When you fast it is like every sense you have is just leaning in to get as close as possible and hear the finest whisper from heaven. In 2004 I was fasting in the lead up to The Call event at the Sydney Showground. I was a few weeks in and really experiencing clarity in hearing God. Over the preceding weeks God had been giving me scriptures to look up that spoke about a change in direction of ministry. I wasn't sure what was happening but just kept pressing in. Then one morning as I was having a prayer time everything shifted. I can remember the moment so clearly. It is one of the defining moments of my life. I was face down on the carpet and experiencing a physical weight of glory on me. Then I heard something from God that was about a clear as I ever had. *In 3 and a half years you are going to plant a church in Bondi Junction.* The clarity was unmistakable. I can remember it to this day as it burned in my heart. God had spoken about the call he had on us. Now as I pounded the pavement of Bondi calling on revival to come I remembered and took heart at the clarity of God speaking.

---

110 THE HOLY BIBLE, NEW INTERNATIONAL VERSION®, NIV® Copyright © 1973, 1978, 1984, 2011 by Biblica, Inc.™

Some people say to me that I would have heard even if I wasn't fasting. They say to me that God would speak anyway. The issue for me however is not so much that God would have spoken anyway but rather would I have been in a position to hear. God is speaking but we are rushing. God is speaking but we are focused elsewhere. God is speaking but we are dulled by a culture of comfort. I know I have heard more life shifting gems from the throne while I fast and pray than any other time of my life.

So the invitation is being extended to you. Just like the early church that would stop and fast and pray and hear direction. God is longing that you sit a while and tune in. He is longing that you take a break from food so your body and spirit can really focus in. You sure know that you need an answer from God about a few things. So why not in the coming weeks block out a few days, get away from the noise, get away from the comfort, get away from the food and empty yourself so God can fill you again. He is wanting to speak, it's just that he isn't always into shouting. Who knows what he might whisper to you. Go ahead and RSVP to the holy invitation of heaven to listen afresh to what the Father wants to say.

# 8.

# INVITATION TO FREEDOM FROM FEAR

All my life I have been worried about what other people think of me. I would be worried that if I don't quite say the right thing or do the right thing then I would be rejected by them in some way. At times it has been paralysing. It has meant being quiet when so many times I should have spoken up. It has meant saving face. It has meant having a private opinion and a public opinion. It has meant being devastated when somebody gives you feedback that is anything short of glowing. It has meant a lot of things but it has all stemmed from a desire to look good and be accepted by people.

During the last couple of years it has become a lot clearer what the dynamic that was operating in my life was called. It was the fear of man. It basically means that the opinion of man is more important to you that the opinion of God. It will cause you to do any thing to keep people happy. Maybe you have experienced it yourself. Holding back advice. Losing sleep over what people will think. Having a church you and a real you. Doing whatever you can to have people speak highly of you and accept you. It all comes from the same root and God wants to bust it off of your life. With it you will never be an effective witness for God. Without it there is no limit to what God can do through you.

A couple of years ago I noticed something had changed after an extended fast I had completed. I didn't notice it the day after or even the week after but rather a couple of months. It happened in a time of receiving some *constructive criticism*. In the past feedback like this used to really rock me. I would go through a low cycle of not wanting to see those people again, anger and just feeling paralysed. However I noticed something different when I was processing these events with my wife, Kate. Something had changed. If I had to scale it I would say that I cared about 50% less than what I had before. I hypothesised that the fasting had brought me to a new level of being free from the fear of man. I didn't have any concrete evidence or even a passage of scripture to base it on but rather just a new level of freedom. So the next couple of fasts I paid special attention to my levels of the fear of man. Each time I finished a fast I noticed a new level of freedom. I can't say for sure if it was because I had a new healthy respect for the opinion of God but I was sure that the fear of man was dying and that these periods of fasting were a positive influence on it.

So with this hypothesis ticking away in the back of my mind I felt God leading me to an Old Testament story that seemed to show the same dynamic. At the time I was preparing for the 2011 National Day of Prayer and Fasting in the Great Hall of Parliament House, Canberra. I was due to share a few thoughts about the importance of Prayer and Fasting. As I prayed God started to share about the fear of man and his desire to break it off. My immediate context was the Christian church and how the Gay Lobby scare many churches into staying silent on gay marriage but the lesson had many applications. The passage God showed me was 1 Kings 19 and the battle between Elijah the prophet and Jezebel. Elijah was ordinarily a man without fear. He had just called fire down on the prophets of Baal and moved with incredible faith and boldness. However, one word from Jezebel and all that changes. He goes from a man on a mission to a man in hiding with the fear of man taken over. 1 Kings 19: 1-3 says

> *Now Ahab told Jezebel everything Elijah had done and how he had killed all the prophets with the sword. So Jezebel sent a messenger to Elijah to say, "May the gods deal with me, be it ever so severely, if by this time tomorrow I do not make your life like that of one of them." Elijah was afraid and ran for his life*[111]

Jezebel issues a death warrant for Elijah's life and he makes a run for it. The boldness he had had in the preceding days immediately disappeared. All that was left was fear so he made a run for it.

Fear has that ability to make us feel like making a run for it. It is one of the primary modes of operation of the kingdom of darkness. It is Satan's most effective weapon besides discouragement in stopping people and the church from rising up and taking what is rightfully theirs. I can really identify with how Elijah must have been feeling. In the early days of moving to Bondi Junction to plant the church Satan would come in my dreams to bully and intimidate me. He would often plant fear in my heart about how things were going to work out. Often Kate and I would say in the first six months of moving *right, that its, we are going home, this is too hard*. It was a spiritual battle of immense proportions. Often we would feel like running for our lives.

So as I read the story of Elijah something jumped out of the text.

---

111 THE HOLY BIBLE, NEW INTERNATIONAL VERSION®, NIV® Copyright © 1973, 1978, 1984, 2011 by Biblica, Inc.™

It says in verse 8 that Elijah ate a meal and then went on the strength of that meal for 40 days and nights. That sounds like a 40 day fast to me. It sounds like a mighty long and powerful fast to me. It sounds like a supernatural fast to me. He didn't plan it but rather the Spirit leads him into a fast that breaks the fear of man off him. In many ways it foreshadows the fast of Jesus as Elijah was out in the wilderness and fasted 40 days. But what happens after this is incredible. The next time we meet Elijah in the narrative he is back to calling down fire and pronouncing judgement over the king. The fear of man is gone and the fear of the Lord is restored.

As God showed me this I knew it was a word for the church in our country. God was saying that he will visit the church with a supernatural fast that will strip off the fear of man and once again restore the fear of the Lord. That the opinion of God would be so much higher than the opinion of any media outlet. In the same way God wants to strip the fear of man off you. Allow him to lead you into a supernatural fast. One that is instigated by him and you are sustained by him. You will never be the same again. You won't recognise yourself. Fear will be decreasing and faith increasing. Go ahead and respond to the holy invitation of the Lord to make you free from fear.

# 9.

# INVITATION TO BE MARKED AS THE BRIDE

Of all the metaphors that Jesus could have used to describe the church as she waits for the second coming, He choose bride. He could have used any collective noun. A troop, a community, a cohort or even a herd. He could have used any of these but yet he didn't because they don't do justice to what he had in mind. He could have used the image of church or gathering but instead it uses an image that evokes such strong emotion. He uses an image that brings ideas of beauty, strength, grace and purity to mind in a powerfully entangled way. There is something about a bride that makes us stop and stare at the sheer beauty.

What Jesus didn't have in mind was a bride that was dirty and torn and limping and half-hearted and just holding on. The bride is an image of beauty. Yet as you look around the *bride* as she is now it can be hard to see that beauty. She is in the process of becoming. The other aspect of the bride that we sometimes miss is that she is full of desire. She is longing to become one with the groom. It is what marks a bride as being set apart from all else. She has an intense desire for the groom to arrive.

It is this intense desire for fulfilment that forms the link with fasting. Whereas in the Old Testament so much of fasting was about mourning, in the New Testament so much of it is about desire for the kingdom and the groom.

Revelation 19 paints a picture of an eschatological feast[112] that we all will celebrate at the final consummation of the Kingdom.[113] It says in verse 6 onwards

> *⁶ Then I heard what sounded like a great multitude, like the roar of rushing waters and like loud peals of thunder, shouting:*
>
> *"Hallelujah!*
> *For our Lord God Almighty reigns.*
> *⁷ Let us rejoice and be glad*
> *and give him glory!*
> *For the wedding of the Lamb has come,*
> *and his bride has made herself ready.*
> *⁸ Fine linen, bright and clean,*
> *was given her to wear."*
> *(Fine linen stands for the righteous acts of God's holy people.)*
>
> *⁹ Then the angel said to me, "Write this: Blessed are those who are invited to the wedding supper of the Lamb!" And he added, "These are the true words of God."* [114]

---

[112] Entry into the Kingdom is compared to admission to a wedding feast in Matthew's gospel at 22:1-14 and 25:1-13.
[113] Scobie, *The ways of our God* 792.
[114] THE HOLY BIBLE, NEW INTERNATIONAL VERSION®, NIV® Copyright © 1973, 1978, 1984, 2011 by Biblica, Inc.™

What really stands out is that it says in this Revelation passage that the bride has made herself ready.

We know for any wedding that happens around us on any given weekend how the Bride makes herself ready. It starts with an early appointment at the hairdressers, followed by a beauty appointment and then followed by the dressing. Some manage a fancy breakfast and champagne and so on. The list of ways to celebrate and get ready are endless. The reality however is that for months the bride has been making herself ready. She has been calling, planning, scheduling and booking for months. All to make this special moment perfect. Months and years of desire and getting ready.

So it is for the Bride of Christ as well. But how does the Bride, the church, make herself ready? We know that this image of the wedding supper was what was in Jesus' mind at Mark 2 when he declares himself the bridegroom. As the bridegroom he states that the need to fast will finally be taken away when the bride is with the bridegroom forever.[115] But in the meantime the mark of the bride is to fast, to long and to desire that the kingdom will come in all its glory and the wedding will take place. I love how Mike Bickle puts it

> *The bridegroom fast is understood and engaged through the focus of this subject called desire. It is understanding His desire, encountering His desire, having our desires fulfilled, enlarging our desires. Desire is the key word if you want to use that or enlarging our spiritual capacities. I like the word desire. In a nut shell He is imparting new desires to us. Desires of delight.... He imparts new desires and that is why the very fact that God makes this available is an awesome privilege to the human race.*

---

115 Lachman, and Smith, (Eds) *Worship in the Presence of God* 267.

> *It is not a drudgery.. it is not the dreaded call to the life of fasting… it is an indescribable privilege because it brings us into new desires of delight. There is nothing that we crave more than to enter into this reality but most people do not know this reality exists and the way to it but the Lord Jesus talks about mourning, longing, panting after a bridegroom in lovesickness.*[116]

This is what Jesus is talking about in Mark 2: 18 when he says he is the groom and the church is the bride. The church period is to be marked by desire. The church with a crazy desire to be with the groom. The church with a crazy desire to be like the groom. This is the radical re-interpretation of fasting that Jesus offers us. Something that transforms us and gets us ready to handle the coming of the Kingdom. Something that transforms the tired and torn into something of strength and beauty. The church across the world is gradually getting this revelation of what it means to become a bride full of desire. A new day is dawning in which the church through a bridal fast is being transformed and made ready. Not only as a thing of beauty and power here but also as all heaven shouts to give God glory as the wedding day approaches.

---

[116] http://thekeyofdavid.wordpress.com/2011/04/22/benefits-of-the-bridegroom-fast/

# 10.

# WHY DON'T WE RSVP?

I can understand when somebody doesn't RSVP to an awkward invitation. Like where you can just sense the person doesn't really want you there. Or you don't really remember them or you feel like you are just making up numbers. I can understand when somebody doesn't RSVP because they have something else on that was planned beforehand or that just plain sounds more interesting. I can understand when somebody doesn't RSVP because the invitation got placed on the fridge door and so it was covered with other invitations and got lost in the mess of life. But I just don't get not RSVPing to the holy invitation that God issues to us to move in more power, to change history, to hear him better and have victory over sin. It doesn't make much sense to me unless there are things actively trying to stop the invitation being heard or causing hesitancy in us RSVPing.

As I consider fasting and the resistance to it I consider a few factor at play that make us really resistant to the idea and cause us not to RSVP.

The first is our cultural dependence on food. Notice I didn't say our physically dependence on food. I didn't deliberately because the two things are quite different. We need food for our bodies to work. No question there. But do we need as much food as we think we need. At the moment the western world is in the grip of an obesity epidemic. We are getting fatter all the time and find it really hard to say no to food. Think about this. For most people, if you miss lunch today nothing bad will happen to you. You will feel hungry but unless you are diabetic, anorexic or sick in some way you are not going to die. Even if you have a raging metabolism you will be OK. But culturally we don't feel like we are going to be OK. We feel like something is wrong. This is a cultural dependence on food. It has incredible power and for the most part goes unquestioned in our thinking. Some of the comments made to me about fasting over the years have been very interesting to think about. They have really displayed to me how culturally dependant we have become. People have said I am crazy and it is wrong to go without. And I wouldn't have disagreed until the moment I went a couple of days without food. I was fine physically but really struggled with the cultural dependence.

It seems to be getting worse as well as our western world turns away from God. In our country over the last couple of years we have seen the *Foodies* movement go from strength to strength. It has given birth to multiple TV shows all with the express aim of elevating food. In our cultural psyche now we are placing more emphasise on food and cooking and making that food something to be desired more than ever. As you watch *Masterchef* you are left feeling that food has become our God as we go to extreme lengths to make the perfect meal. Don't get me wrong, I love great food, its just I refuse to let it be everything to me.

The other aspect of this type of love of food is the way that it comforts us. We joke about chocolate being the classic comfort food but really all food can be comfort food if we are eating for the wrong reasons. Ask yourself this next time you are depressed or anxious about something. Am I eating to give my body the fuel it needs or am I eating to make myself feel better. Again I don't want to be a wowser. I love eating yummy things. I think God made them for our enjoyment. But if we head straight for those foods in a time of crisis then we short change ourselves. God wants to be our first port of call when we are stressed or depressed or anxious and not the fridge. This has become so established in our culture now that we don't even mentally process it. If you were to keep a mood and food diary you might be shocked at the trigger points we have for eating. There is no doubt that eating makes people feel happy. So many times as I break a fast I feel the warm contentedness of that food reaching my stomach but God wants to be everything to us. I don't want us not to RSVP to this invitation because we have fallen to the lie of the media and fast food outlets that you can't survive without. The truth is you can survive and as you hunger and thirst for righteousness you will be filled with something so much better that nobody can take it away.

Another reason we tend not to RSVP concerning the holy invitation to fast has to do with out theology. I grew up in a good protestant church and let me tell you the idea of lent is not a very popular idea at all in the protestant church. To most Protestants lent is perceived as a work of trying to gain grace. The typical language that is used around the idea is that lent is the *gospel plus* something else in order to be righteous. When a practice such as fasting and lent are used in such terms it can be really hard to celebrate them because you tend to be on the back foot in having to defend why you do them. The reality about fasting however is that it has nothing to do with gaining grace or favour with God. It is all about indentifying with Jesus and the forty day fast he did and putting away good things in order to draw close to the saviour. The protestant church needs to be very careful about labelling spiritual disciplines that have been helpful down the ages as *gospel plus.* Just because a practice has been helpful in drawing close to God does not mean that the person practicing it thinks it is the means of grace. Fasting often makes me highly aware of grace but never causes me to think by it I have gained grace.

Another theological reason why some do not **RSVP** is that of our understanding of the will of God. If you believe that every single event, both personally and corporately that happens is because it is the will of God then the whole concept of prayer and fasting is thrown into question. There becomes no need to pray because God wills every single event and there is nothing we can do about this. An old ordained minister friend of mine once told me of the destructiveness of this doctrine on a local parish level. He told me of churches he had worked in and presently did in which prayer was really questioned. It seemed like the passion for prayer had left because the purpose of it was undervalued. Jesus however had no such theology. When asked how to pray he responded with this in Matthew 6

> *Our Father in heaven,*
> *hallowed be your name,*
> *your kingdom come,*
> *your will be done,*
>   *on earth as it is in heaven.*[117]

Jesus' theology was that there was only one place in which the perfect will of God was being done and that was in heaven and the role of the people on earth was to pray that the perfect will of God in heaven would become an earthly reality as well. John's preamble to Jesus in verse 13 of chapter one gives us an idea that there are completing wills. He says of the birth of Jesus, that it wasn't about the will of man or a husband but rather that Jesus was born so much as it was because of the will of

---

117 THE HOLY BIBLE, NEW INTERNATIONAL VERSION®, NIV® Copyright © 1973, 1978, 1984, 2011 by Biblica, Inc.™

God. No, to say that God wills every single event is to say that God wills people to sin and we know that this is simply not correct. It is the will of man that causes man to sin. So according to Jesus our mandate is that we pray the perfect will of God into the situations we face here on earth. It is like every event of sin is a holy invitation for people to pray and fast for deliverance and redemption to break out.

In my thinking there seems to be one more reason that causes us not to RSVP. That is the issue of passivity. In Australia we have a great saying. It is *She'll be right*. It simply means not to give to much thought to something because it is going to work itself out in the end. It comes from a pretty passive national mindset and encourages passivity. While it sums up a relaxed attitude to problems which can be helpful in terms of not panicking, it can cause a person or nation to do little in the face of destruction. I can imagine that if Joel 2 was given directly to Australia we would say to Joel *No worries mate, she'll be right* which is exactly the opposite response that the prophet Joel is looking for. He is looking for action and intervention. There comes a time when a nation, city, people group, church or family have to say that it is not going to be business as usual. It is not going to be a time in which things just take their *natural* course. It is going to be a time of rising up and partnering with God to release his perfect will into any and all situations in which we find on planet earth. But it isn't going to take just one or two here and there rising up against business as usual. It is going to take an army. An army of people who know who they are and what God has called them to do and the weapons he has put into their hands. It is going to take an uprising of global proportions to see this world turned around and God's kingdom released into every nook and cranny.

So why not RSVP? Why not RSVP today? I know that before I did I was nervous but now I look back on it as one of the best decisions I have ever made. I have experienced empowerment I never knew existed. I have experienced God speaking so clearly. I have experienced such freedom from fear. Now it is your turn to respond to the holy invitation that is being issued from heaven.

# BIBLIOGRAPHY

Achtemeier, E. *Minor Prophets I N.I.B.C.* (Peabody, Mass.: Hendrickson Publishers, 1996).

Allen, L. C. *The books of Joel, Obadiah, Jonah and Micah NICOT* (London : Hodder & Stoughton, 1976).

Allen, P., Canning, R. and Cross, L. (Eds) *Prayer and Spirituality in the Early Church. Volume 1* (Everton Park, Qld: Centre for Early Christian Studies, Australian Catholic University, 1998).

Barnett, Paul *The Servant King : reading Mark today.* (Sydney: Anglican Information Office, 1991).

Ben Ezra, D. S. *Whose Fast is it?* in Becker, A. H. and Reed, A. Y. (Eds) *The ways that never parted: Jews and Christians in late antiquity and the early Middle Ages* (Minneapolis, Minn.: Fortress Press, 2007).

Black, M. *Fast of Feasten?* History Today, April 81, Vol. 31 Issue 4, p58

Blunt, A. W. F. *Fasting* in Hastings, J; Selbie, J. A.; Lambert, J. C.; Mathews, S. (Eds) *Dictionary of the Bible* (Peabody, Mass. : Hendrickson Publishers, 1989).

Bock, D. L., Luke. *Volume 1. 1:1 - 9:50.* (Grand Rapids, Mich. Baker Books, 1994).

Bock, D. L., *Gospel of Luke* in Reid, D. G. (Ed), *The IVP Dictionary of the New Testament* (Illinois USA.: IVP, 2004).

Buksbazen, V. *The Gospel and the Feasts of Israel.* (W. Collingswood, N.J: Spearhead Press, 1972).

Busenitz, I. A. *Joel and Obadiah* (Great Britain: CFP, 2003).

Calvin, J. *A harmony of the Gospels Matthew, Mark and Luke. Volume 1 translator, A. W. Morrison* (Grand Rapids, Mich.: William B. Eerdmans, 1980).

Chatham, R. D. *Fasting: A Biblical Historical Study* (Bridge-Logos Publishers, 1987).

Chisholm, R. B. *Interpreting the Minor Prophets* (Grand Rapids, Mich.: Zondervan Publishing House, 1990).

Cranfield, C.E.B. *The Gospel according to Saint Mark* (Cambridge, Eng.: Cambridge University Press, 1959).

Crump, D. *Knocking on Heaven's Door: a New Testament theology of petitionary prayer* (Grand Rapids, Mich.: Baker Academic, 2006).

Daise, M. A. *Feasts in John: Jewish festivals and Jesus' 'hour' in the Fourth Gospel* (Tubingen, Germany: Mohr Siebeck, 2007).

H. A. G. B., Fasting in Douglas, J.D. *New Bible Dictionary* (Leicester, U.K: Inter-Varsity Press, 1985).

Duffy, E. *To Fast Again* First Things, no 151 March 2005, p 4-6

Enns, P. *The Moody Handbook of* Theology (Chicago: Moody Press, 1989).
Foster, R. *Celebration of Discipline* (London: Hodder and Stoughton, 1989).

France, R.T. *Gospel of Mark: a commentary on the Greek text.* NIGTC (Grand Rapids, Mich.: William B. Eerdmans, 2002).

Frykholm, A. J. *Soul food.* Christian Century, 3/8/2005, Vol. 122 Issue 5, p24-27.

Garland, D. E. *Mark in Zondervan Illustrated Bible backgrounds commentary* (Grand Rapids, Mich.: Zondervan, 2002).

Garrett, D. A. *Hosea, Joel. New American commentary* (U.S.A: Broadman & Holman, 1997).

Grabbe, L. L. *I Cried to the Lord: A Study of the Psalms of Solomon's Historical Background and Social Setting.* Journal for the Study of the Old Testament, June 2005, Vol. 29 Issue 5, p177.

Grady, T. *Lent in the fast lane.* U.S. Catholic, March 2002, Vol. 67, Issue 3.

Green, J. B. *The Gospel of Luke. NICNT* (Grand Rapids, Mich.: William B. Eerdmans, 1997).

Grudem, W. *Systematic Theology* (Bath, England: IVP, 1994).

Grun, A. *Fasting* in Fahlbusch, E. (Ed) *The encyclopaedia of Christianity* (Marshallton, Del.: National Foundation for Christian Education, 1964-1972).

Guelich, R. A. *Mark. Word Biblical commentary* (Dallas, Tex.: Word Books, 1989).

Gundry, R. H. *A Survey of the New Testament* (Grand Rapids USA; Zondervan, 1981).

Haartman, K. *Watching and Praying: personality transformation in eighteenth century British Methodism* (Amsterdam: Rodopi, 2004).

Harrington, D. J. *To Fast or not to Fast* America, 2/20/2006, Vol. 194 Issue 6, p30

Houston, J. A. *Prayer: the transforming friendship* (Oxford, Eng.: Lion, 1993).

Hubbard, D. A. *Joel and Amos: an introduction and commentary* (Leicester, Eng.: Inter-Varsity Press, 1989).

Kostenberger, A. J. *Encountering John,* (Grand Rapids: Baker, 1999).

Lachman, D. and Smith, F. J. (Eds) *Worship in the Presence of God* (Greenville, S.C.: Greenville Seminary Press, 1992).

Lambert, D. A. *Fasting* in Sakenfeld, K. D. (Ed) *The New Interpreter's dictionary of the Bible* (Nashville, Tenn.: Abingdon, 2006).

Lancaster, T. D. *New Wine and Old Wineskins: The Parable of Luke 5:36-39 Re-examined* (http://www.bethimmanuel.org/) accessed on 23/10/2008

Levering, M. *On Prayer and Contemplation: classic and contemporary text* (Lanham, Md.: A Sheed & Ward Book, 2005).

Marshall, I. H. *Jesus-Example and Teacher of Prayer in the Synoptic Gospels* in Longnecker, R. N. (ed.) *Into God's Presence: Prayer in the New Testament* (Grand Rapids, Mich.: William B. Eerdmans, 2001).

Louth, A. *Fasting* in Hastings, A., Mason, A. and Pyper, H. (Eds) *The Oxford companion to Christian thought* (New York: Oxford University Press, 2000).

McComiskey, T. E. *The Minor Prophets: an exegetical and expository commentary. Volume 1: Hosea, Joel and Amos* (Grand Rapids, Mich.: Baker Book House, 1992).

Mentzer, R. A. *Fasting, piety, and political anxiety among French Reformed Protestants* Church History, 76 no 2 Je 2007, p 330-362.

Merrill, E. H. *Fasting* in Elwell, W. A., *Evangelical dictionary of theology* (Grand Rapids, Mich.: Baker Book House, 1984).

Muddiman, J. *Fasting* in Freedman, D. N. *The Anchor Bible dictionary* (New York: Doubleday, 1992).

Nolland, J. *Luke 1 - 9:20. Word Biblical commentary* (Dallas, Tex.: Word Books, 1989).

Oswalt, J. N. *The Book of Isaiah: Chapters 40-66* (Grand Rapids, USA: Eerdmans Pub. Co., 1998)

Patterson, B. *Christianity Today*; 03/02/98, Vol. 42 Issue 3, p48.

Piper, J. *A Hunger for God: Desiring God through Fasting and Prayer* (USA: Crossway Books, 1997).

Plymale, S. F. *The prayer texts of Luke-Acts.* (New York: Peter Lang, 1991).

Prince, D. *Shaping History through Prayer and Fasting* (England: Whitaker House, 2002).

Robertson, O. P. *Prophet of the coming day of the Lord: the message of Joel.* (Durham, NC: Evangelical Press, 1995).

Rothenberg, F. S. *Fast* in Brown, C. (Ed) *The new international dictionary of New Testament theology* (Exeter, Eng.: Paternoster, 1975-1978).

Ryan, T. *Fasting: A Fresh Look.* America, 3/6/2006, Vol. 194 Issue 8, p8-12,

Scobie, C. H. H. *The ways of our God* (Grand Rapids, Mich.: William B. Eerdmans, 2003).

Smith, D. R., *Fasting: a neglected discipline.* (London: Hodder & Stoughton, 1974).

Smith-Christopher, D. L. *Fasting* in Freedman, D. N.; Myers, A. C. (Ed) *Eerdmans dictionary of the Bible* (William B. Eerdmans, Grand Rapids, Mich.: 2000).

Stein, R. H. *Luke. NAC* (Nashville, Tenn.: Broadman Press, 1992).

Tamney, J. B. *Fasting and Dieting* Review of Religious Research, 27 no 3 March 1986, 255-263.

Tamney, J. B. *Fasting and modernization.* Journal for the Scientific Study of Religion, 19 no 2 Je 1980, p 129-137.

Twelftree, G. H. *Temptation of Jesus* in Green. J. B. and McKnight, S. (Eds) *Dictionary of Jesus and the Gospels* (Downers Grove, Ill.: IVP, 1992).

Vaage, L. E. and Wimbush, V. L. (Eds), *Asceticism and the New Testament* (New York: Routledge, 1999).

Westermann, C. *Isaiah 40-66* (Philadelphia, Pa.: Westminster Press, 1987).

Whybray, R.N. *Isaiah 40-66 NCBC* (Grand Rapids, Mich.: William B. Eerdmans, 1981).

# ABOUT THE AUTHOR

Matt is passionate about many things. About his wife and four kids. About revival coming to Australia. About world missions. About new generations finding Jesus. About his favourite sporting teams. About swimming at the beach and about ordinary people doing extraordinary things.

Facebook: www.facebook.com/matt.madigan
Smashwords: www.smashwords.com/profile/view/MattMadigan

www.ingramcontent.com/pod-product-compliance
Lightning Source LLC
LaVergne TN
LVHW051506070426
835507LV00022B/2958